Limbic Resonance

When Two Minds Share the Same Emotional Frequency in a World of Static

Aubrey Shepherd

Limbic Resonance

Chapter 1: Understanding Limbic Resonance

The Evolution of Emotional Connection

Emotional connections have undergone significant transformations throughout human history, shaped by cultural shifts, technological advances, and changing social structures. The journey of how humans form and maintain emotional bonds reveals fascinating patterns that continue to evolve in our modern world.

Ancient societies prioritized emotional connections within tight-knit communities, where survival often depended on strong interpersonal bonds. These early emotional frameworks laid the groundwork for how we understand attachment and belonging today. Archaeological evidence suggests that even prehistoric humans created elaborate rituals and ceremonies to strengthen emotional ties within their groups.

The agricultural revolution marked a crucial shift in emotional connection patterns. As communities became more settled, new forms of emotional bonds emerged, tied to land ownership and extended family structures. These connections often spanned generations, creating deep-rooted emotional inheritances that some cultures still maintain.

Medieval periods saw emotional connections heavily influenced by religious and social hierarchies. Courtly love emerged as a complex system of emotional expression, while family bonds remained primarily practical rather than affectionate. However, personal letters from this era reveal surprisingly tender emotional expressions that challenge our assumptions about historical relationships.

The industrial revolution dramatically altered how people formed and maintained emotional connections. Urban migration separated families, while new social structures created novel opportunities for emotional bonding beyond traditional family units. Factory workers formed strong emotional ties through shared experiences, developing support systems that transcended blood relations.

Victorian era attitudes introduced new complexities to emotional expression. While public displays of emotion became increasingly regulated, private emotional lives grew richer and more nuanced. The rise of the novel as a popular form allowed people to explore emotional depths previously unacknowledged.

The 20th century brought unprecedented changes to emotional connection patterns. World wars created intense bonds between soldiers while disrupting traditional family structures. The post-war period saw the emergence of youth culture, introducing new ways of forming emotional connections outside family and community frameworks.

Modern technology has revolutionized how we create and maintain emotional bonds. Social media platforms offer unprecedented opportunities for connection while simultaneously challenging traditional concepts of emotional intimacy. Research indicates that digital communications can both enhance and complicate emotional relationships.

Contemporary workplace environments have become significant sites for emotional connection. Professional relationships often blur traditional boundaries between personal and professional bonds, creating complex emotional landscapes that require careful navigation.

Global mobility has introduced new patterns of emotional connection maintenance. Long-distance relationships, once considered nearly impossible, have become commonplace, supported by communication technologies that allow for regular emotional expression across vast distances.

Psychological research reveals how emotional connection patterns adapt to changing circumstances. Studies show that humans continuously develop new strategies for forming and maintaining emotional bonds in response to environmental and social changes.

Cultural fusion in modern societies has led to hybrid forms of emotional expression and connection. Traditional practices merge with contemporary approaches, creating rich new ways of building and sustaining emotional relationships.

The role of shared experiences in emotional connection has evolved significantly. While physical presence remains important, virtual shared experiences increasingly contribute to emotional bond formation and maintenance.

Children's emotional development patterns show marked changes in recent decades. Early exposure to diverse connection forms influences how younger generations approach emotional relationships and express their feelings.

Professional therapeutic approaches to emotional connection have evolved substantially. Modern mental health practices recognize the importance of cultural context and individual differences in emotional expression and attachment styles.

Community structures continue to adapt, creating new frameworks for emotional connection. Urban planning increasingly considers the importance of social spaces that facilitate emotional bonding among residents.

Educational systems now acknowledge the crucial role of emotional intelligence in human development. Schools incorporate social-emotional learning, preparing students for more complex emotional landscapes in their future lives.

Research into neurological aspects of emotional connection reveals how brain structure and function influence bonding patterns. This understanding helps explain why certain connection forms persist while others evolve.

Environmental factors increasingly impact emotional connection patterns. Climate change and environmental concerns create new forms of shared emotional experience and collective response.

Future trends suggest continuing evolution in how humans form and maintain emotional connections. Emerging technologies and changing social structures will likely introduce novel forms of emotional bonding while preserving essential human needs for connection.

The acceleration of social change indicates that emotional connection patterns will continue to evolve rapidly. However, core human needs for meaningful emotional bonds remain constant, even as expression forms change.

Understanding this evolution helps individuals navigate contemporary emotional landscapes more effectively. Recognition of how connection patterns have changed allows for more intentional approaches to building and maintaining emotional relationships.

The ongoing transformation of emotional connection reflects humanity's remarkable adaptability. As we face new challenges and opportunities, our capacity for meaningful emotional bonds continues to evolve while remaining fundamentally essential to human experience.

The Neuroscience Behind Limbic Systems

Limbic systems represent one of the most fascinating and complex neural networks in the human brain, orchestrating emotions, memories, and behavioral responses that shape our daily experiences. Located deep within the brain, this intricate collection of structures works in harmony to process and regulate our emotional lives.

The amygdala, often described as the emotional sentinel of the brain, plays a crucial role in processing fear and pleasure responses. Consider Sarah, a mountain climber who experiences both terror and exhilaration during her ascents. Her amygdala rapidly processes these competing emotions, helping her make split-second decisions that ensure her safety while allowing her to pursue her passion.

Hippocampal function within the limbic system demonstrates remarkable sophistication in memory formation and emotional context integration. Recent studies reveal how this seahorse-shaped structure creates neural patterns that link emotions to specific memories, explaining why certain songs can instantly transport us back to significant life moments.

The cingulate cortex serves as a crucial bridge between emotional and cognitive processes. Neuroimaging studies show increased activity in this region when individuals navigate complex social situations or experience moral conflicts. This understanding has revolutionized our approach to treating emotional regulation disorders.

Hypothalamic functions within the limbic system coordinate our physiological responses to emotional states. When David experiences workplace stress, his hypothalamus triggers a cascade of hormonal responses, affecting everything from his heart rate to his digestive processes. Understanding these mechanisms helps develop more effective stress management techniques.

The fornix, a C-shaped bundle of nerve fibers, facilitates crucial communication between different limbic structures. Research demonstrates how damage to this pathway can significantly impact emotional memory formation and recall, highlighting its importance in maintaining emotional well-being.

Thalamic involvement in limbic processing reveals sophisticated filtering mechanisms for sensory information. This neural gateway helps determine which external stimuli receive emotional attention, explaining why we might remain calm during a thunderstorm but jump at an unexpected tap on the shoulder.

The nucleus accumbens plays a central role in reward processing and motivation. Studies of this structure have transformed our understanding of pleasure-seeking behaviors and addiction, revealing how emotional rewards shape our decision-making processes.

Neuroplasticity within limbic structures demonstrates remarkable adaptability. Through repeated experiences and conscious effort, individuals can reshape their emotional responses, creating new neural pathways that support healthier emotional patterns.

Hormonal interactions with limbic structures create complex feedback loops that influence emotional states. Understanding these interactions has led to breakthrough treatments for mood disorders and anxiety conditions.

The orbitofrontal cortex's role in emotional regulation showcases the sophisticated interplay between rational thought and emotional response. This region helps us modify our emotional reactions based on social context and personal goals.

Neurotransmitter systems within the limbic network operate with remarkable precision. Serotonin, dopamine, and norepinephrine work in concert to modulate emotional states and influence behavioral responses.

Developmental aspects of limbic system maturation explain age-related differences in emotional processing. Adolescents' heightened emotional responses stem from ongoing limbic system development, providing crucial insights for educational and parenting approaches.

Stress responses orchestrated by limbic structures demonstrate evolutionary adaptation. Understanding these ancient survival mechanisms helps develop more effective approaches to managing modern stressors.

The role of limbic systems in social bonding reveals fascinating neural mechanisms. Oxytocin release, regulated by limbic structures, facilitates attachment and trust, fundamentally influencing human relationships.

Sleep's impact on limbic function shows critical connections between rest and emotional regulation. During sleep, these neural networks process emotional experiences and consolidate emotional memories.

Environmental influences on limbic system development highlight the importance of early experiences. Childhood environments significantly shape these neural circuits, affecting long-term emotional processing patterns.

Research into limbic system dysfunction has revolutionized mental health treatment approaches. Understanding neural mechanisms behind emotional disorders leads to more targeted therapeutic interventions.

Exercise effects on limbic function demonstrate the powerful connection between physical activity and emotional well-being. Regular movement promotes healthy limbic system operation through various neurochemical pathways.

Meditation's influence on limbic structures reveals how conscious practices can modify emotional processing. Brain imaging studies show significant changes in limbic activity among long-term meditation practitioners.

Nutritional impacts on limbic function underscore the importance of diet in emotional health. Specific nutrients directly affect neurotransmitter production and limbic system operation.

Genetic factors in limbic system development explain individual differences in emotional processing. Understanding these variations helps create personalized approaches to emotional regulation.

The integration of limbic function with other brain systems demonstrates remarkable complexity. This neural orchestra works continuously to create our emotional experience while maintaining physiological balance.

Modern research techniques continue revealing new aspects of limbic system operation. Each discovery deepens our understanding of human emotional experience and provides new opportunities for promoting psychological well-being.

The Role of Mirror Neurons

Mirror neurons represent one of the most remarkable discoveries in neuroscience, fundamentally changing our understanding of human behavior, empathy, and social learning. These specialized brain cells fire both when we perform an action and when we observe others performing the same action, creating a neural bridge between self and other experiences.

Consider a young child watching her mother prepare dinner. As her mother chops vegetables, the child's mirror neurons activate in patterns similar to if she were holding the knife herself. This neural mimicry forms the foundation for learning complex skills and understanding others' intentions.

Research has shown that mirror neurons play a crucial role in emotional contagion - the phenomenon where one person's emotions and associated behaviors directly trigger similar emotions and behaviors in other people. When you see someone smile, your mirror neurons activate, often prompting you to smile in return, even before conscious awareness.

The impact of mirror neurons extends far beyond simple motor actions. Studies reveal their involvement in understanding others' intentions and emotional states. When Sarah observes her friend John reaching for a glass of water, her mirror neurons help her understand not just the physical action, but also John's underlying intention to quench his thirst.

Professional athletes utilize mirror neuron systems during training. Watching expert performances triggers neural patterns that help improve their own execution of complex movements. This explains why observational learning proves so effective in sports training and skill development.

Language acquisition heavily relies on mirror neuron function. Children learn speech patterns by observing mouth movements and linking them to sounds, with mirror neurons creating internal representations of these actions. This process facilitates both understanding and reproduction of language.

Artists and musicians particularly benefit from mirror neuron activity. When a pianist watches another musician perform, their mirror neurons fire in patterns matching the observed finger movements, strengthening neural pathways for their own playing.

Social bonding mechanisms depend significantly on mirror neuron function. These cells help us synchronize our behaviors with others, creating the foundation for empathy and cooperative behavior. Group activities become more coordinated through this unconscious neural mimicry.

Cultural learning relies heavily on mirror neuron systems. Traditional customs, social norms, and behavioral patterns transfer between generations through observation and neural mirroring, maintaining cultural continuity while allowing for gradual evolution.

Therapeutic applications of mirror neuron understanding have revolutionized rehabilitation practices. Stroke patients show improved recovery when therapy includes observation of normal movement patterns, activating mirror neurons to support motor relearning.

Dance and movement therapies leverage mirror neuron function to promote emotional healing. Watching and mimicking expressive movements triggers emotional resonance through mirror neuron activation, facilitating psychological processing and recovery.

Parent-child relationships benefit from healthy mirror neuron function. Infants learn emotional regulation by observing and internally mimicking their caregivers' responses, building fundamental social-emotional skills through neural mirroring.

Educational settings can optimize learning by incorporating mirror neuron principles. Teachers who demonstrate concepts while explaining them engage students' mirror neurons, enhancing understanding and retention through multiple neural pathways.

Empathy development strongly correlates with mirror neuron activity. These cells help us literally feel what others feel, creating the neural basis for compassionate responses and social understanding.

Leadership effectiveness often relates to mirror neuron engagement. Successful leaders naturally activate followers' mirror neurons through consistent, authentic behavior patterns that others unconsciously emulate.

Creative processes benefit from mirror neuron function. When artists observe others' creative works, their mirror neurons fire, stimulating new neural connections that enhance their own creative expression.

Social anxiety may involve altered mirror neuron activity. Understanding this connection helps develop more effective treatments focusing on normalizing social signal processing through mirror neuron engagement.

Team dynamics improve when mirror neuron function is considered. Activities that promote synchronized movement or shared experiences strengthen group cohesion through enhanced neural mirroring.

Conflict resolution benefits from understanding mirror neuron roles. When mediators model calm, solution-focused behavior, participants' mirror neurons support adoption of similar approaches.

Personal development accelerates through conscious use of mirror neuron principles. Surrounding oneself with individuals demonstrating desired behaviors activates supportive neural patterns through mirroring.

Professional communication improves with awareness of mirror neuron effects. Speakers who effectively engage audiences' mirror neurons through authentic expression achieve better connection and message retention.

Relationship building strengthens through mirror neuron activation. Genuine interest and attention to others triggers reciprocal neural patterns, creating stronger social bonds through unconscious mirroring.

Future research continues revealing new aspects of mirror neuron function, promising deeper understanding of human social behavior and learning processes. Each discovery offers new opportunities for applying these insights to enhance human development and interaction.

The profound influence of mirror neurons on human behavior and social connection underscores their fundamental importance in shaping our experiences and relationships. Understanding and consciously working with these neural mechanisms can significantly enhance personal and professional growth.

Emotional Contagion and Social Bonding

Emotional contagion operates as a fundamental force in human interaction, spreading feelings and moods through groups like invisible ripples across a pond. This remarkable phenomenon shapes our social connections, influences group dynamics, and plays a crucial role in how we form and maintain relationships.

When Sarah walked into her office one morning radiating enthusiasm, her positive energy quickly spread among her colleagues. Within hours, the entire department's atmosphere had shifted, demonstrating how one person's emotional state can transform group dynamics. This natural process occurs through subtle facial expressions, body language, and vocal tones that we unconsciously mimic and internalize.

Research reveals that emotional contagion begins in infancy, where babies mirror their caregivers' facial expressions and emotional states. This early bonding mechanism establishes neural pathways that continue influencing our social connections throughout life. Studies show that infants as young as three months old demonstrate this synchronization with their caregivers' emotions.

The workplace serves as a particularly potent environment for emotional contagion. Leaders' moods significantly impact team performance and satisfaction. A manager's stress or confidence spreads rapidly through their team, affecting productivity, creativity, and collaboration. Understanding this dynamic helps organizations cultivate more positive work environments.

Social gatherings amplify emotional contagion effects. Whether at a concert, sports event, or religious ceremony, collective emotions emerge as individuals synchronize their emotional states. This shared emotional experience strengthens group bonds and creates lasting social connections.

Close relationships intensify emotional contagion. Couples often experience mood synchronization, where one partner's emotional state directly influences the other's. This emotional mirroring can strengthen relationship bonds but also requires awareness to maintain healthy boundaries.

Digital communication has introduced new patterns of emotional contagion. Social media platforms spread emotional states across vast networks, creating waves of collective feeling that can influence social movements and public opinion. Research indicates that online emotional contagion operates similarly to in-person experiences.

Cultural differences affect emotional contagion patterns. Some societies encourage emotional expression and sharing, while others value emotional restraint. These cultural norms influence how emotions spread within communities and shape social bonding practices.

Physical proximity enhances emotional contagion effects. Working in shared spaces, living together, or participating in group activities increases emotional synchronization. This explains why remote teams often struggle to maintain the same level of emotional connection as co-located groups.

Stress transmission through emotional contagion presents particular challenges in healthcare settings. Medical professionals must balance empathy with emotional boundaries to prevent burnout while maintaining therapeutic relationships with patients.

Educational environments demonstrate powerful emotional contagion effects. Teachers' enthusiasm or anxiety directly influences student engagement and learning outcomes. Understanding this dynamic helps educators create more effective learning environments.

Athletic teams rely on emotional contagion for performance enhancement. A single player's confidence or determination can elevate the entire team's performance through emotional synchronization. Coaches leverage this phenomenon to build team cohesion.

Family systems experience intense emotional contagion. Children particularly absorb parental emotions, highlighting the importance of emotional awareness in family relationships. This understanding helps parents create healthier emotional environments for child development.

Therapeutic settings utilize emotional contagion principles for healing. Group therapy sessions harness collective emotional experiences to facilitate individual growth and recovery. Therapists carefully manage group dynamics to promote positive emotional contagion.

Professional negotiations benefit from understanding emotional contagion. Skilled negotiators consciously manage their emotional state, knowing it will influence other participants' attitudes and decisions. This awareness can lead to more successful outcomes.

Public speaking effectiveness depends heavily on emotional contagion. Speakers who genuinely connect with their emotions more successfully engage audiences through natural emotional transmission. This authentic connection creates lasting impact.

Community organizations strengthen social bonds through shared emotional experiences. Group activities, celebrations, and collective challenges create opportunities for positive emotional contagion that builds community resilience.

Romantic relationships thrive on healthy emotional contagion. Partners who maintain positive emotional states while respecting individual emotional boundaries create stronger, more sustainable connections.

Crisis situations intensify emotional contagion effects. Understanding this helps emergency responders maintain calm and focus while managing challenging situations. Their emotional stability can help stabilize affected populations.

Creative collaborations benefit from emotional contagion. Artists working together often experience shared emotional states that enhance creative flow and artistic expression. This synchronization can lead to remarkable creative achievements.

Leadership development programs increasingly incorporate emotional contagion awareness. Effective leaders learn to consciously manage their emotional impact on others while fostering positive group dynamics.

The power of emotional contagion in social bonding reveals our deep interconnectedness. By understanding and consciously working with these natural processes, we can create stronger relationships and more positive social environments. This awareness enables more effective leadership, stronger communities, and healthier relationships across all aspects of life.

The Chemistry of Connection

Chemical messengers in our bodies orchestrate an intricate dance that shapes our connections with others, influencing everything from first impressions to lifelong bonds. These molecular interactions create the biological foundation for human relationships, affecting our emotions, behaviors, and social choices in profound ways.

Oxytocin, often called the bonding hormone, plays a central role in human connection. When Sarah held her newborn for the first time, a surge of oxytocin flooded her system, initiating a powerful bond that would shape both their lives. This same molecule strengthens romantic relationships, friendships, and even trust between strangers.

Dopamine creates the excitement we feel in new relationships. That flutter in your stomach when meeting someone special comes from dopamine release, motivating us to pursue meaningful connections. Research shows that even brief eye contact with someone we're attracted to can trigger a dopamine response, explaining the chemistry of attraction.

Serotonin levels significantly influence our social behavior and emotional well-being. When David started his morning routine of jogging with friends, his elevated serotonin levels improved not only his mood but also his social interactions throughout the day. Regular social exercise creates a positive feedback loop of chemical rewards.

Endorphins strengthen social bonds through shared experiences. Groups of friends who exercise together, laugh together, or overcome challenges as a team experience synchronized endorphin release, creating lasting neural associations with these social connections.

Cortisol, the stress hormone, plays a complex role in relationships. While acute stress can initially draw people closer, chronic elevation of cortisol can damage relationships. Understanding this balance helps people manage stress in ways that protect their connections with others.

Norepinephrine contributes to social alertness and attraction. That heightened awareness you feel in the presence of someone special stems from this molecule's effects. It sharpens our focus and makes social interactions more memorable.

Vasopressin works alongside oxytocin to promote long-term bonding. Studies show its particular importance in male pair-bonding behaviors, influencing fidelity and paternal care. This hormone helps explain why stable relationships contribute to overall well-being.

Phenylethylamine creates the euphoria of new love. Remember that light-headed feeling of falling in love? This chemical messenger generates the excitement and encrgy characteristic of romantic attraction, though its effects typically moderate as relationships mature.

Beta-endorphins released during social touch reinforce human connections. A warm hug or friendly pat on the back triggers these natural opioids, explaining why physical contact plays such a crucial role in maintaining relationships.

Testosterone and estrogen balance influences social behavior patterns. These sex hormones affect everything from mate selection to parenting styles, shaping how we form and maintain relationships throughout our lives.

Prolactin promotes caregiving behaviors beyond just parent-child relationships. Its presence helps explain why we feel compelled to care for friends in need or support struggling colleagues.

GABA (Gamma-Aminobutyric Acid) helps regulate social anxiety. When functioning optimally, this neurotransmitter allows us to feel calm and confident in social situations, facilitating deeper connections.

Adrenaline can enhance social bonding through shared exciting experiences. Couples who engage in thrilling activities together often report stronger relationships, thanks to the chemical cocktail of excitement and attraction.

Pheromones, though subtle in humans, influence social preferences and attraction. These chemical signals operate below conscious awareness yet affect our social choices and relationships.

The gut microbiome produces chemicals that affect social behavior. Recent research reveals how bacterial balance influences mood and social interaction patterns through the gut-brain axis.

Cannabinoid receptors in our bodies respond to social reward similarly to other pleasurable experiences. This system helps explain why positive social interactions feel naturally rewarding.

Acetylcholine supports social memory formation and emotional learning. Strong social memories depend on this neurotransmitter's proper function, helping us maintain long-term relationships.

Growth factors like BDNF (Brain-Derived Neurotrophic Factor) strengthen social learning and adaptation. Regular social interaction promotes the release of these molecules, supporting brain health and social capability.

Inflammatory markers affect social behavior and bonding. Managing inflammation through lifestyle choices can improve social connections by optimizing our chemical balance.

Melatonin's rhythm influences social timing and synchronization. Healthy sleep patterns supported by this hormone improve social interaction quality and emotional regulation.

Understanding these chemical mechanisms empowers us to make choices that support healthy relationships. Regular exercise, adequate sleep, healthy diet, and positive social interactions create an optimal chemical environment for connection.

The intricate interplay of these chemicals demonstrates how deeply relationships affect our physical well-being. By nurturing our social connections, we support not just our emotional health but our entire physiological system.

This chemical orchestra plays continuously throughout our lives, influencing every interaction and relationship we experience. Recognizing these biological foundations helps us appreciate the profound importance of human connection while guiding us toward choices that enhance our relationships and overall well-being.

Chapter 2: The Symphony of Shared Emotions

Emotional Frequencies and Brain Waves

Brain waves and emotional states interweave in an intricate dance, creating distinct patterns that reflect our inner experiences and shape our interactions with the world. These neural oscillations, measured in different frequencies, correspond directly to various emotional states and levels of consciousness.

Delta waves, the slowest brain frequencies at 0.5-4 Hz, emerge predominantly during deep sleep and profound meditation. Sarah discovered that during her deepest grief following her father's passing, her brain produced intense delta activity, reflecting an internal healing process similar to deep sleep restoration.

Theta waves, occurring at 4-8 Hz, manifest during emotional processing and creative inspiration. Artists often report entering theta states while creating, experiencing a dreamlike consciousness where emotions flow freely into their work. These waves play a crucial role in emotional memory formation and intuitive understanding.

Alpha waves, ranging from 8-13 Hz, represent a bridge between emotional awareness and calm clarity. When Michael practices mindful breathing, his brain produces strong alpha waves, creating a state of relaxed alertness that allows him to process emotions without becoming overwhelmed.

Beta waves, at 13-30 Hz, dominate our normal waking consciousness and active problem-solving states. During heated emotional discussions, increased beta activity reflects heightened engagement and emotional arousal. However, excessive beta can indicate anxiety or emotional stress.

Gamma waves, the fastest at 30-100 Hz, correlate with peak emotional experiences and states of heightened awareness. Musicians report intense gamma activity during performances when feeling deeply connected to their music and audience, suggesting these waves' role in profound emotional experiences.

Research reveals that emotional trauma can disrupt normal brain wave patterns, creating irregular frequencies that contribute to emotional difficulties. Understanding these patterns helps therapists develop more effective treatments using neurofeedback and other brain-based approaches.

Meditation practitioners demonstrate remarkable control over their brain wave patterns, able to shift between frequencies intentionally. This skill enables better emotional regulation and deeper emotional awareness, showing how conscious practice can influence neural oscillations.

Love and attachment generate unique brain wave signatures. When couples in long-term relationships make eye contact, their brain waves often synchronize, particularly in the alpha and theta ranges, demonstrating the neural basis of emotional connection.

Fear and anxiety typically produce high-frequency beta waves, sometimes disrupting lower-frequency patterns necessary for emotional processing. Learning to shift into alpha and theta states through breathing exercises or meditation can help manage these challenging emotions.

Children's developing brains show different emotional frequency patterns than adults. Their greater theta wave activity explains their vivid emotional experiences and creative imagination, offering insights into emotional development.

Social interactions create complex patterns of brain wave synchronization between individuals. Group activities like singing or dancing together can align participants' brain waves, explaining the emotional bonding that occurs in collective experiences.

Grief counselors observe that processing loss involves cycles through different brain wave states. The healing journey includes periods of delta-wave restoration, theta-wave emotional processing, and beta-wave integration of the experience.

Athletes in "the zone" display unique combinations of alpha and gamma waves, reflecting both relaxed focus and peak performance. This state allows for optimal emotional regulation during high-pressure situations.

Sleep plays a crucial role in emotional processing, with different sleep stages characterized by distinct wave patterns. During REM sleep, theta waves help integrate emotional experiences, explaining why sleep disruption can impact emotional stability.

Creative breakthrough moments often occur during transitions between brain wave states. Artists report their best ideas emerging when shifting from beta to alpha states, highlighting the relationship between neural oscillations and emotional inspiration.

Empaths and highly sensitive individuals often show more pronounced theta wave activity, possibly explaining their heightened emotional awareness and sensitivity to others' feelings. This understanding helps them manage their unique emotional experiences more effectively.

Environmental factors influence brain wave patterns and corresponding emotional states. Natural settings tend to promote alpha wave activity, explaining why time in nature often feels emotionally restorative.

Technology use typically increases beta wave activity, potentially contributing to emotional overstimulation. Regular breaks and practices that promote alpha and theta states can help balance these effects.

Emotional healing often involves restoring healthy brain wave patterns. Trauma survivors show improved emotional regulation when their brain wave patterns normalize through targeted interventions.

Age-related changes in brain wave patterns affect emotional processing throughout life. Understanding these changes helps develop appropriate emotional support strategies for different life stages.

The relationship between emotional frequencies and brain waves reveals the intricate connection between our neural activity and emotional experiences. This understanding opens new pathways for emotional healing, personal growth, and enhanced relationships through conscious awareness of our brain states and their emotional correlates.

The Language Beyond Words

Silent conversations unfold constantly around us, carrying messages that often speak louder than words ever could. A slight tilt of the head, a subtle shift in posture, or a fleeting facial expression can convey volumes of information that transcend verbal communication.

Consider Maria, who immediately sensed her friend's distress despite the cheerful words being spoken. The slightly hunched shoulders, downturned mouth corners, and lack of eye contact told the real story. This innate ability to read nonverbal cues develops from infancy, when babies first learn to interpret their caregivers' facial expressions and body language.

Gestures serve as a universal language that crosses cultural boundaries. While specific gestures may carry different meanings across cultures, the basic human tendency to communicate through movement remains constant. Research shows that even congenitally blind individuals use similar gestures while speaking, suggesting an innate connection between movement and communication.

Micro-expressions flash across faces in fractions of seconds, revealing genuine emotions before conscious control can mask them. These brief facial movements prove particularly valuable in understanding others' true feelings. Paul Ekman's groundbreaking research identified seven universal facial expressions: happiness, sadness, anger, fear, surprise, disgust, and contempt.

Proxemics, the study of personal space, reveals how physical distance communicates relationship dynamics. Observe any social gathering, and you'll notice people unconsciously adjusting their positions to maintain comfortable distances based on their relationships and cultural norms.

Touch carries profound meaning in human interaction. A firm handshake, a gentle pat on the back, or a warm hug can communicate support, authority, or affection more effectively than words. The timing, pressure, and duration of touch all contribute to its meaning.

Paralinguistics encompasses vocal elements beyond words themselves. Tone, pitch, volume, and pace of speech convey emotional states and attitudes. A simple "hello" can communicate dozens of different meanings through variations in these vocal qualities.

Eye contact patterns reveal attention, interest, and emotional connection. While cultural norms influence appropriate eye contact duration, the eyes consistently serve as powerful communicators of internal states. Pupil dilation, blink rate, and gaze direction all carry specific meanings.

Posture broadcasts confidence, submission, or engagement levels. A person's physical alignment can immediately communicate their emotional state and attitude toward others. Standing tall with shoulders back projects confidence, while slouching often indicates discomfort or disengagement.

Clothing and appearance choices communicate social status, personality, and intentions. Color selections, style choices, and grooming habits send messages about identity and desired social interactions. These choices often speak before any verbal exchange occurs.

Environmental arrangements reflect and influence communication patterns. The positioning of furniture, the use of space, and the selection of objects all contribute to nonverbal messaging. Consider how a room's setup can encourage or discourage interaction.

Chronemics, the study of time's role in communication, reveals how timing and punctuality convey respect and power dynamics. Arriving early, exactly on time, or late each sends distinct messages about the relationship and relative status of participants.

Silence itself communicates powerfully. The strategic use of pauses can emphasize points, demonstrate thoughtfulness, or express disapproval. Different cultures attribute varying meanings to silence, but its communicative power remains universal.

Body orientation reveals attention and attitude. The direction people face, whether their bodies are open or closed, and how they position themselves relative to others all convey meaningful information about relationships and intentions.

Facial feedback influences emotional experiences. The act of smiling, even when forced, can generate positive feelings, demonstrating the bidirectional relationship between expression and emotion.

Mirror neurons activate when we observe others' actions and expressions, creating internal simulations that help us understand others' experiences. This biological mechanism underlies our capacity for empathy and nonverbal understanding.

Authentic versus performed nonverbal communication shows distinct patterns. Genuine expressions involve whole-face engagement, while forced expressions often appear asymmetrical or poorly timed.

Cultural differences in nonverbal communication highlight the importance of context in interpretation. What's appropriate or meaningful in one culture may carry different implications in another, requiring careful attention to cultural norms.

Technology has introduced new forms of nonverbal communication through emojis, reaction buttons, and timing indicators. These digital signals attempt to replace the rich nonverbal cues lost in online interaction.

The mastery of nonverbal communication enhances personal and professional relationships. Understanding and consciously managing nonverbal signals improves leadership effectiveness, relationship quality, and personal influence.

Reading and responding to nonverbal cues requires practice and awareness. Developing this skill enables deeper connections and more effective communication across all aspects of life. The language beyond words continues to shape our interactions, relationships, and understanding of one another in profound ways.

Synchronized Hearts and Minds

Hearts and minds operate in remarkable synchrony, creating patterns of connection that extend far beyond individual experience. When two people share a profound moment, their physiological rhythms begin to align in ways that science is only beginning to understand.

Sarah and James discovered this phenomenon during their first dance as a married couple. As they moved together, their heart rates synchronized, their breathing patterns aligned, and their neural activity began to mirror each other's. This wasn't merely romantic coincidence – research has documented how close physical proximity and shared emotional experiences create measurable biological synchronization.

Studies of parent-child relationships reveal that mothers and infants naturally synchronize their heartbeats when making eye contact. This biological harmony supports emotional bonding and helps regulate the infant's developing nervous system. Even more fascinating, this synchronization occurs at a distance of up to three feet, suggesting an electromagnetic component to human connection.

Musicians performing together demonstrate remarkable neural synchrony. When an orchestra plays in perfect harmony, the musicians' brain waves align, creating a shared neural network that enhances their collective performance. This same phenomenon appears in successful business teams, where members develop synchronized cognitive patterns during collaborative problem-solving.

Couples who have been together for years often finish each other's sentences not just because they know each other well, but because their neural patterns have become intertwined through years of shared experience. Research shows that long-term partners develop similar brain response patterns when viewing emotional content, suggesting a deep level of cognitive alignment.

The phenomenon of emotional contagion demonstrates how feelings spread through groups, creating synchronized emotional states. Whether in a concert crowd, a protest march, or a meditation retreat, people naturally align their emotional frequencies when sharing significant experiences.

Physical touch accelerates this synchronization process. Hold hands with someone you trust, and within minutes, your heart rates begin to harmonize. This biological synchrony explains why touch can be so comforting during times of distress – it literally helps regulate our physiological state through connection with another's steady rhythm.

Meditation practitioners who practice together show remarkable synchronization in brain wave patterns. This shared state enhances the meditation experience and creates a sense of collective consciousness that participants often describe as transcendent.

Athletic teams in peak performance demonstrate synchronized movement patterns and shared anticipatory responses. Basketball players anticipate their teammates' movements through a combination of visual cues and developed neural synchrony, allowing for split-second coordination.

The phenomenon extends to larger groups as well. Audiences at compelling performances often show synchronized heart rates and breathing patterns, especially during emotional peaks in the performance. This collective physiological response enhances the shared experience and creates lasting social bonds.

Teachers and students develop subtle synchronization during effective learning experiences. When engagement is high, their brain activity patterns align, facilitating better information transfer and deeper understanding.

Crisis situations can trigger rapid synchronization among emergency responders. Their shared focus and coordinated responses emerge from both training and natural biological alignment under pressure.

Even in digital interactions, people show signs of physiological synchronization. Video calls, while not as powerful as in-person contact, can still create measurable alignment in conversation partners' responses and rhythms.

The quality of synchronization often reflects relationship health. Couples with strong emotional connections show more stable and consistent physiological alignment than those experiencing relationship difficulties.

Group rituals and ceremonies harness this synchronizing power. Whether in religious services, cultural celebrations, or community gatherings, shared movements and experiences create powerful collective states.

Leadership effectiveness correlates with the ability to create physiological synchrony. Charismatic leaders naturally entrain their followers' biological rhythms, creating a sense of connection that enhances influence and trust.

Nature itself provides rhythms that humans naturally synchronize with. The 24-hour circadian cycle, seasonal changes, and even lunar phases influence our biological patterns and social connections.

Understanding these synchronization mechanisms offers practical applications. Therapists use this knowledge to better attune to their clients, while negotiators learn to create physiological alignment to build trust and agreement.

The development of empathy relies partly on this capacity for biological synchronization. As we attune to others' states, our own physiology shifts to match theirs, creating

the biological foundation for understanding and
compassion.

Modern technology often disrupts natural synchronization
patterns. Awareness of this effect helps us make conscious
choices about when to disconnect from devices and
reconnect with direct human contact.

The future of human connection lies in understanding and
cultivating these natural synchronization processes. As we
face increasing challenges requiring collective action, our
ability to achieve deep synchrony with others becomes ever
more crucial.

This remarkable capacity for hearts and minds to
synchronize reminds us of our fundamental
interconnectedness. By fostering conditions that support
natural biological alignment, we enhance our relationships,
improve group performance, and create more meaningful
shared experiences.

Chapter 3: Navigating the Static
Modern Barriers to Emotional Connection

Digital screens cast their blue glow across millions of faces each day, creating an invisible wall between genuine human connections. What began as tools for enhanced communication have evolved into barriers that fundamentally alter how we relate to one another emotionally.

Rachel noticed it during a family dinner when all four of her children sat hunched over their phones, responding with delayed, half-hearted answers to her questions. The warmth of traditional family gatherings had been replaced by the cold comfort of digital distraction. This scene repeats itself countless times across homes worldwide, highlighting a growing emotional disconnect in our modern era.

Social media platforms promise connection but often deliver comparison and anxiety instead. Users scroll through carefully curated highlights of others' lives, measuring their own experiences against unrealistic standards. This constant comparison creates emotional exhaustion and diminishes authentic self-expression.

The workplace has transformed into a landscape of virtual meetings and instant messages, where subtle emotional cues get lost in transmission. Body language, micro-expressions, and the natural rhythm of face-to-face conversation disappear behind screens, making it harder to build genuine professional relationships.

Time scarcity poses another significant barrier. Modern schedules packed with commitments leave little room for spontaneous interactions or deep conversations. People rush through social encounters, checking phones between sentences, never fully present in any single moment.

Urban design often prioritizes efficiency over community, creating physical spaces that discourage meaningful interaction. High-rise apartments with closed doors, busy streets without gathering spaces, and neighborhoods without walkable areas all contribute to social isolation.

The culture of busyness has become a status symbol, making it socially acceptable to avoid emotional engagement. "I'm too busy" serves as a shield against vulnerability, preventing deeper connections from forming.

Fear of judgment in an era of constant documentation leads many to maintain carefully controlled public personas. The knowledge that any interaction might be recorded and shared creates hesitation in expressing genuine emotions or taking social risks.

Remote work, while offering flexibility, has eliminated the casual conversations and spontaneous collaborations that build workplace relationships. Water cooler moments, once crucial for emotional bonding, have disappeared from many professional lives.

Overreliance on text-based communication strips away emotional nuance. Tone, timing, and context get lost in translation, leading to misunderstandings and emotional distance. Even emoji and reaction buttons prove poor substitutes for genuine emotional expression.

The attention economy fragments our focus, making it difficult to maintain the sustained attention necessary for meaningful connection. Notifications constantly pull us away from present moments, disrupting the flow of natural conversation.

Privacy concerns in the digital age create barriers to openness. Awareness of data collection and potential surveillance makes people hesitant to share genuine thoughts and feelings, even in seemingly private conversations.

The decline of community institutions removes traditional spaces for emotional connection. Religious gatherings, community centers, and local events that once brought people together regularly have diminished in many areas.

Individualistic cultural values emphasize self-reliance over interdependence, making it harder to acknowledge emotional needs or seek support from others. This cultural shift creates invisible barriers to vulnerability and connection.

The fast pace of modern life leaves little time for emotional processing. People move quickly from one experience to another without fully integrating their emotional responses, leading to superficial connections.

Geographic mobility, while offering opportunities, disrupts long-term relationships and community ties. Frequent moves for career advancement often come at the cost of sustained emotional connections.

The commodification of social interaction through apps and services creates transactional relationships where authentic emotional connection once flourished. Dating apps, networking platforms, and social media metrics reduce human connection to measurable data points.

Information overload creates emotional numbness. Constant exposure to global tragedies and crisis news can overwhelm our capacity for empathy, making it harder to connect emotionally with others' experiences.

Age segregation in modern society limits intergenerational connections. Separate spaces for different age groups reduce opportunities for emotional learning and support across generations.

The pressure to maintain a digital presence consumes energy that might otherwise go toward nurturing real-world relationships. Managing online personas and interactions can feel like a full-time job, leaving little capacity for deeper connections.

Understanding these barriers represents the first step toward overcoming them. By recognizing how modern life structures inhibit emotional connection, we can make conscious choices to create space for authentic relationships. The challenge lies not in eliminating these barriers entirely, but in developing strategies to maintain genuine human connection despite them.

Digital Age Disconnection

Screens illuminate faces in dark rooms across the globe, casting an ethereal glow that masks a growing void in human connection. The digital revolution promised to bring people closer together, yet paradoxically, it has created unprecedented levels of isolation and emotional distance.

Mark noticed the shift gradually in his teenage daughter Emma. Once vivacious and engaging during family dinners, she now sits silently, thumbs dancing across her phone screen, responding to messages from friends who sit equally alone in their own homes. The physical presence of family has been replaced by the constant pull of virtual connections.

Research reveals disturbing trends in social behavior since the widespread adoption of smartphones. Average eye contact during conversations has decreased by 40% in the past decade, while reported feelings of loneliness have reached epidemic proportions. Young adults, despite being more connected than ever through social media, report higher rates of social anxiety and isolation than previous generations.

The phenomenon of "phubbing" - snubbing others by focusing on phones - has become so commonplace that many no longer notice its impact on relationships. Couples sit across restaurant tables, both absorbed in separate digital worlds, while their untouched meals grow cold between them.

Virtual interactions have replaced crucial developmental experiences for younger generations. Children who once learned conflict resolution through playground negotiations now manage disagreements through text messages, missing essential lessons in reading facial expressions and body language.

The dopamine-driven feedback loops of social media create addictive patterns that override natural social instincts. Each notification, like, and comment triggers small bursts of pleasure that pale in comparison to genuine human connection, yet prove more compelling through their immediate accessibility.

Sleep patterns suffer as devices emit blue light late into the night, disrupting circadian rhythms and the natural social synchronization that occurs in households. Family members operate on increasingly disconnected schedules, reducing opportunities for meaningful interaction.

Public spaces have transformed into seas of downturned faces. Train commutes once filled with casual conversations or shared observations now pass in digital silence. The subtle art of reading social cues atrophies as fewer practice the skill of striking up conversations with strangers.

Work relationships suffer as remote technology replaces office interactions. While video calls maintain basic communication, they fail to capture the energy of collaborative creativity that sparks when people share physical space. The nuanced understanding that develops through informal workplace interactions diminishes in virtual environments.

Dating has evolved into a gamified experience where potential partners are reduced to swipeable profiles. The rich complexity of human attraction gets filtered through algorithms, while the chemistry of in-person meetings becomes an increasingly rare experience.

Parents struggle to model healthy technology use while managing their own digital dependencies. Children learn by example, yet find few role models for balanced engagement with digital tools. Family dynamics shift as devices compete for attention previously devoted to shared activities and conversations.

The concept of presence has fundamentally changed. Being physically present no longer implies emotional or mental availability. People increasingly exist in multiple spaces simultaneously, their attention fractured between physical reality and virtual engagements.

Social skills show marked decline as digital communication becomes the primary mode of interaction. Basic abilities like maintaining eye contact, reading social cues, and engaging in unstructured conversation become challenging for those who rarely practice these skills in person.

Memory formation suffers when experiences are filtered through devices. Rather than fully engaging with moments, people focus on documenting them for social media, creating a generation of observers rather than participants in their own lives.

The constant availability of entertainment and distraction eliminates natural periods of boredom that once sparked creativity and social connection. Waiting rooms, bus stops, and quiet moments that once fostered spontaneous interactions now pass in isolated screen time.

Digital boundaries blur work and personal life, creating a state of constant partial attention. The ability to truly disconnect becomes increasingly rare as professional and social obligations demand continuous availability.

Empathy decreases as people consume carefully curated versions of others' lives. The raw, authentic moments that build genuine understanding become increasingly rare in a world where everything is filtered and edited before sharing.

The solution lies not in wholesale rejection of digital technology but in conscious recalibration of its role in our lives. Creating device-free spaces and times, prioritizing face-to-face interactions, and developing healthy digital boundaries can help restore balance to increasingly disconnected lives.

Recognition of digital disconnection as a significant social issue marks the first step toward change. By understanding how technology shapes our relationships and conscious choices about its use, we can begin to rebuild the deep connections that make us fundamentally human.

The challenge ahead involves learning to harness digital tools without letting them dominate our social experiences.

Future generations must develop new skills for maintaining genuine human connection in an increasingly virtual world.

Emotional Interference Patterns

Emotions ripple through our lives like waves, creating complex interference patterns that shape our relationships and experiences. These patterns emerge from the intersection of different emotional frequencies, much like waves in a pond when multiple stones are dropped simultaneously.

Maria discovered this phenomenon during a family gathering where her joy at seeing her children collided with anxiety about her mother's declining health. The resulting emotional turbulence left her feeling disconnected from both experiences, unable to fully embrace either emotion. This common occurrence demonstrates how emotional interference patterns can diminish our capacity to process feelings authentically.

Research in emotional psychology reveals that when multiple strong emotions occur simultaneously, they create interference patterns that can either amplify or cancel each other out. Like sound waves that combine to create harmony or dissonance, emotional waves interact in ways that profoundly affect our psychological well-being.

Workplace scenarios often generate complex interference patterns. A promotion might trigger both excitement and impostor syndrome, creating an emotional standing wave that paralyzes decision-making. These competing feelings can create internal conflict that affects performance and relationships with colleagues.

Romantic relationships particularly demonstrate these patterns. The excitement of new love can interfere with fear of vulnerability, creating emotional turbulence that manifests as mixed signals or inconsistent behavior. Partners often struggle to navigate these interference patterns, leading to misunderstandings and communication breakdowns.

Childhood experiences create baseline emotional frequencies that continue to influence adult relationships. When these deep-seated patterns intersect with current situations, they can amplify reactions beyond what present circumstances warrant. A minor criticism at work might trigger disproportionate emotional responses rooted in early experiences of failure or rejection.

Social gatherings illuminate how emotional interference patterns operate in groups. One person's anxiety can create ripples that interact with another's excitement, generating complex group dynamics that affect everyone present. Understanding these patterns helps explain why certain combinations of people create harmony while others produce tension.

Grief provides a powerful example of emotional interference. The sadness of loss often collides with unexpected moments of joy or gratitude, creating confusion and guilt. These interference patterns explain why grief rarely progresses in a linear fashion but instead moves in waves of varying intensity.

Cultural expectations add another layer to emotional interference patterns. Societal norms about appropriate emotional expression can create interference with authentic feelings, leading to suppression or displacement of genuine emotions. This interference often manifests as stress-related physical symptoms.

Family systems demonstrate how emotional patterns transmit across generations. Children unconsciously adopt their parents' emotional frequencies, creating interference patterns that persist into adulthood. Breaking these patterns requires conscious awareness and deliberate effort to establish new emotional resonances.

Personal growth often involves navigating complex interference patterns between desired change and comfortable habits. The excitement of potential transformation collides with fear of the unknown, creating resistance that must be understood rather than fought against.

Professional relationships showcase how power dynamics create emotional interference. The desire to speak truthfully might conflict with fear of consequences, generating patterns of communication that obscure rather than clarify meaning.

Time management challenges often stem from emotional interference patterns. The urgency of immediate tasks collides with the importance of long-term goals, creating paralysis or scattered attention. Understanding these patterns helps in developing more effective strategies for prioritization.

Creative processes particularly suffer from emotional interference. Self-doubt can create patterns that interfere with inspiration, while perfectionism generates waves that cancel out the natural flow of ideas. Recognizing these patterns allows artists and innovators to work with rather than against their emotional currents.

Decision-making becomes complicated when multiple emotional frequencies compete for attention. The rational assessment of options can be overwhelmed by interference from fears, desires, and unconscious biases. Awareness of these patterns improves the quality of important life choices.

Relationship conflicts often escalate due to unrecognized interference patterns. What begins as a simple disagreement can amplify through the interaction of past hurts, current stresses, and future fears. Understanding these dynamics enables more constructive approaches to conflict resolution.

Health and wellness efforts frequently encounter emotional interference. The desire for healthy change collides with comfort-seeking behaviors, creating patterns that undermine good intentions. Success in lifestyle modifications requires addressing these underlying emotional dynamics.

Learning to navigate emotional interference patterns represents a crucial life skill. Like a skilled sailor reading wave patterns, we can learn to recognize and work with emotional currents rather than being overwhelmed by them.

This understanding enables more authentic relationships and more effective personal development.

The key lies not in eliminating interference patterns, which exist naturally in any complex emotional system, but in developing awareness and skills to work with them constructively. By recognizing these patterns in ourselves and others, we can create more harmonious relationships and more fulfilling lives.

The Price of Emotional Isolation

Silent rooms echo with unspoken feelings as millions endure the growing burden of emotional isolation. The cost manifests not only in mental health statistics but in the subtle erosion of human connection that shapes our society's fabric.

Sarah recognized the price one Sunday afternoon when she realized she hadn't spoken to another person in three days. Despite hundreds of social media connections and a busy professional life, genuine emotional exchanges had become rare gems in her daily experience. Her story reflects a widespread phenomenon that health researchers increasingly link to concerning physical and psychological outcomes.

Studies reveal that emotional isolation carries a health impact equivalent to smoking fifteen cigarettes daily. The body responds to emotional disconnection by increasing stress hormones, inflammation markers, and blood pressure. These physiological changes accumulate over time, accelerating aging and increasing susceptibility to various diseases.

The workplace bears witness to this costly phenomenon. Productivity suffers as emotionally isolated employees struggle with motivation and creativity. Companies report higher turnover rates and increased healthcare costs among workers who lack strong social connections. The financial impact extends beyond individual organizations to affect entire economic systems.

Children growing up in emotionally isolated environments demonstrate delayed social development and struggle with emotional regulation. Their academic performance often suffers, not from lack of intelligence but from missing the emotional security that enables effective learning. These early deficits can echo throughout their lives, affecting future relationships and career prospects.

Relationships deteriorate when emotional isolation becomes normalized within families. Partners stop sharing vulnerable moments, parents miss crucial emotional cues from their children, and siblings grow distant despite living under the same roof. The cost compounds as these patterns repeat across generations.

Mental health professionals report increasing cases of anxiety and depression linked to emotional isolation. Traditional treatment methods prove less effective when patients lack the social support systems necessary for recovery. The healthcare system strains under the weight of treating symptoms while struggling to address the root cause.

Urban planning decisions inadvertently contribute to the problem. Modern cities designed for efficiency often sacrifice community spaces that historically facilitated emotional connection. The resulting environment reinforces isolation, creating a feedback loop that makes meaningful interaction increasingly rare.

The elderly population bears a particularly heavy burden. As traditional family structures change and communities become more transient, older adults often find themselves cut off from emotional support systems. Their physical health deteriorates more rapidly without regular emotional engagement, leading to increased healthcare costs and reduced quality of life.

Professional success, once believed to compensate for emotional isolation, proves an inadequate substitute. High-achieving individuals report feeling empty despite their accomplishments, discovering too late that career advancement cannot fill the void left by meaningful connection.

Cultural shifts toward independent living carry hidden costs. While celebrating self-sufficiency, society overlooks the essential role of emotional interdependence in human well-being. The resulting isolation manifests in rising rates of substance abuse, self-harm, and other maladaptive coping mechanisms.

The digital economy profits from emotional isolation while exacerbating it. Social media platforms and entertainment services capitalize on lonely individuals seeking connection, offering temporary relief while deepening the underlying problem. This economic model creates powerful incentives to maintain rather than solve the isolation crisis.

Romantic relationships suffer as people lose the skills necessary for emotional intimacy. Dating becomes a surface-level exercise in compatibility checking rather than a genuine exploration of connection. The resulting partnerships often lack the emotional depth necessary for long-term satisfaction.

Community organizations report declining participation as emotional isolation becomes normalized. Religious institutions, social clubs, and volunteer organizations struggle to maintain membership, further reducing opportunities for meaningful connection. The social fabric weakens with each lost gathering space.

Healthcare costs soar as the physical manifestations of emotional isolation require treatment. Chronic conditions, autoimmune disorders, and stress-related illnesses increase in prevalence, straining medical resources without addressing the underlying cause.

Educational systems face mounting challenges as emotionally isolated students struggle with basic social skills. Teachers report spending increasing time managing social-emotional issues rather than academic content. The long-term implications for workforce readiness and social cohesion remain concerning.

The environmental impact compounds as isolated individuals seek comfort in consumption rather than connection. The resulting pattern of resource use adds ecological costs to the already high price of emotional isolation.

Recovery from this crisis requires acknowledging its true cost and implementing systemic changes. Communities must prioritize creating opportunities for genuine connection, while individuals learn to value and nurture emotional bonds. The price of continuing current patterns proves too high for sustainable human flourishing.

Understanding these costs represents the first step toward change. By recognizing emotional isolation as a public health crisis rather than a personal choice, society can begin developing effective interventions. The investment in rebuilding human connection, while significant, pales in comparison to the ongoing price of emotional isolation.

Finding Signal in the Noise

Amidst the constant barrage of information, discerning meaningful signals from background noise has become a crucial survival skill. Like a radio operator fine-tuning frequencies in search of clear transmission, modern humans must develop the ability to filter through endless streams of data to find what truly matters.

David, a journalist with twenty years of experience, noticed his ability to spot authentic stories diminishing as social media floods his feeds with sensational headlines. His journey to rediscover genuine signals amid the noise reflects a universal struggle in our information-saturated world.

Research indicates that the human brain processes an average of 34 gigabytes of information daily, compared to just 2 gigabytes thirty years ago. This exponential increase in data input creates cognitive overload, making it increasingly difficult to identify meaningful patterns and essential information.

Professional environments suffer particularly from noise pollution. Endless email chains, chat notifications, and meeting requests create a cacophony that drowns out important signals about project progress, team dynamics, and strategic opportunities. Productivity plummets as workers struggle to maintain focus amid the chaos.

Personal relationships face similar challenges. Genuine emotional signals get lost in the static of social media updates, emoji reactions, and superficial digital interactions. Partners miss crucial nonverbal cues while drowning in a sea of text messages and notifications.

The marketplace of ideas has become increasingly noisy, with valid information competing against misinformation and deliberate disinformation. Critical thinking skills prove essential yet insufficient when facing sophisticated techniques designed to manipulate attention and perception.

Natural intuition, once a reliable guide for detecting important signals, becomes overwhelmed by artificial stimuli designed to trigger emotional responses. The resulting confusion leads many to either shut down completely or accept all input without discrimination.

Sleep patterns suffer as the brain struggles to process the day's information overflow. Dreams, nature's way of sorting signal from noise, become fragmented and less effective at integrating experiences and emotions. The resulting sleep deficit further impairs cognitive filtering abilities.

Educational systems face the challenge of teaching students to identify reliable sources while developing resilience against information overload. Traditional research skills require updating for an era where quantity of information no longer correlates with quality or truth.

Cultural shifts occur as societies lose shared reference points amid competing narratives. Communities fragment into echo chambers, each generating its own noise while filtering out signals that challenge established beliefs. The resulting polarization further complicates the search for truth.

Scientific discovery increasingly requires sophisticated tools to detect meaningful signals within massive datasets. Yet human intuition remains crucial for identifying which patterns deserve deeper investigation. The balance between technological assistance and human discernment defines modern research.

Financial markets demonstrate how noise can overwhelm even experienced professionals. Day-to-day price fluctuations create static that obscures underlying economic signals. Successful investors develop strategies to filter out market noise while remaining alert to significant indicators.

Creative processes require protection from the constant barrage of input. Artists and innovators must cultivate quiet spaces where genuine inspiration can emerge above the background noise of trending topics and viral content.

Health monitoring becomes challenging as individuals navigate conflicting medical advice and health trends. The signal of one's own body often gets lost amid noise from fitness apps, wellness influencers, and contradictory research headlines.

Environmental awareness suffers when immediate distractions drown out signals of long-term change. Climate scientists struggle to communicate crucial data through the noise of daily news cycles and competing political narratives.

Professional development requires increasingly sophisticated filtering mechanisms. Career opportunities and genuine networking connections hide within a flood of LinkedIn updates and job listings. Success depends on developing reliable methods for identifying meaningful signals.

Meditation and mindfulness practices gain importance as tools for clearing mental static. Regular periods of quiet allow the brain to reset its filtering mechanisms and rediscover natural rhythms of attention and focus.

Time management transforms into attention management as individuals learn to protect their cognitive bandwidth. Calendar blocking and notification settings become crucial tools for controlling input and maintaining space for important signals to emerge.

The solution lies not in complete isolation from information but in developing better filtering systems. Like noise-canceling headphones, effective strategies reduce background static while allowing important signals through. This requires conscious choice about information sources and regular assessment of filtering methods.

Success in the modern world increasingly depends on the ability to find signal in noise. Those who develop this skill gain significant advantages in professional advancement, personal relationships, and overall well-being. The challenge remains maintaining these filtering systems while staying open to unexpected signals that might carry important messages.

Understanding the difference between signal and noise becomes an essential life skill, one that requires constant refinement as information channels multiply. The future belongs to those who master this fundamental aspect of modern existence.

Chapter 4: The Art of Emotional Attunement

Developing Emotional Awareness

Emotional awareness forms the cornerstone of personal growth and meaningful relationships, yet many people navigate life with limited understanding of their emotional landscape. Like an artist learning to distinguish subtle shades of color, developing emotional awareness requires practice, patience, and dedication.

Rachel discovered this truth during a pivotal moment in her career when a colleague's simple question - "How are you feeling about the project?" - left her stammering. Despite her professional success, she realized she had spent years operating on autopilot, disconnected from her emotional responses to daily experiences.

Research in neuroscience reveals that emotional awareness activates specific brain regions associated with self-understanding and empathy. When people actively engage with their emotions, these neural pathways strengthen, leading to improved emotional regulation and interpersonal relationships.

Physical sensations often provide the first clues to emotional states. A tightening chest might signal anxiety, while a fluttering stomach could indicate excitement or nervousness. Learning to recognize these bodily signals helps identify emotions before they become overwhelming.

Childhood experiences significantly influence emotional awareness development. Family environments that acknowledge and validate feelings create strong foundations for emotional intelligence. However, those raised in households where emotions were dismissed or punished often require focused effort to rebuild these connections.

Workplace settings present unique challenges for emotional awareness. Professional expectations of constant composure can lead to emotional suppression, making it difficult to recognize and process feelings appropriately. Progressive organizations now recognize that emotional awareness contributes to better decision-making and leadership.

Relationships flourish when partners develop strong emotional awareness. The ability to identify and communicate feelings creates deeper intimacy and reduces misunderstandings. Couples who practice emotional awareness report higher satisfaction and better conflict resolution skills.

Journal writing serves as a powerful tool for developing emotional awareness. The act of describing emotional experiences in writing helps clarify subtle feelings and recognize patterns in emotional responses. Regular journaling creates a valuable record of emotional growth over time.

Cultural factors influence emotional awareness development. Some societies emphasize emotional expression while others value restraint. Understanding these cultural contexts helps individuals navigate their emotional development while respecting their heritage.

Body language reveals much about emotional states, yet many people remain unaware of their non-verbal communication. Learning to recognize physical manifestations of emotions in oneself and others enhances emotional awareness and improves social interactions.

Sleep quality significantly impacts emotional awareness. Well-rested individuals demonstrate better ability to identify and process emotions compared to those experiencing sleep deprivation. Prioritizing sleep becomes essential for maintaining emotional clarity.

Creative activities often bypass intellectual barriers to emotional awareness. Art, music, and movement can access feelings that words struggle to capture. Engaging in creative expression provides valuable insights into emotional states.

Stress management directly relates to emotional awareness. Understanding personal stress responses helps identify emotional triggers and develop effective coping strategies. This awareness prevents emotional overwhelm during challenging situations.

Professional relationships benefit from increased emotional awareness. Leaders who understand their emotional responses make more balanced decisions and create healthier work environments. Team dynamics improve when members possess strong emotional awareness.

Physical exercise contributes to emotional awareness development. Movement helps release stored emotions and creates space for clearer emotional perception. Regular exercise supports overall emotional well-being and awareness.

Time alone proves essential for developing emotional awareness. Quiet reflection allows subtle emotions to surface and be recognized. Creating regular solitude helps maintain connection with one's emotional state.

Social support plays a crucial role in emotional awareness development. Trusted friends and mentors provide valuable feedback and help validate emotional experiences. Building a supportive network enhances emotional growth.

Nature connection facilitates emotional awareness. Time outdoors often clarifies emotional states and provides perspective on internal experiences. Regular nature exposure supports emotional development and awareness.

Meditation practices strengthen emotional awareness by creating space to observe feelings without judgment. Regular meditation develops the capacity to recognize and understand emotional states more clearly.

Professional guidance through therapy or counseling can accelerate emotional awareness development. Trained professionals help identify blind spots and provide tools for deeper emotional understanding.

The digital age presents unique challenges to emotional awareness. Constant connectivity and information overload can dull emotional sensitivity. Intentional breaks from technology help maintain emotional clarity.

Success in developing emotional awareness requires commitment to regular practice. Like any skill, emotional awareness grows stronger with consistent attention and effort. The benefits extend far beyond personal growth to enhance all aspects of life.

Understanding emotions creates freedom from their unconscious influence. As emotional awareness develops, choices become more conscious and aligned with authentic desires. This awareness forms the foundation for meaningful personal transformation.

The journey of emotional awareness continues throughout life, offering new insights and deeper understanding with each experience. Embracing this ongoing process creates rich opportunities for growth and connection in all relationships.

The Practice of Present Connection

Connection to the present moment remains one of humanity's most elusive yet vital pursuits. Modern life constantly pulls attention toward future anxieties or past regrets, while the rich texture of immediate experience slips by unnoticed.

Mark discovered this truth during a routine morning commute when his young daughter pointed at a magnificent rainbow he had completely missed while checking emails.

That moment sparked a fundamental shift in his approach to daily life, leading him to explore the profound impact of present connection.

Research indicates that people spend nearly 47% of their waking hours thinking about something other than their current activity. This mental wandering significantly reduces life satisfaction and increases stress levels. The ability to maintain present connection directly correlates with reported happiness levels and relationship satisfaction.

Physical sensations provide an anchor to the present moment. The feeling of breath moving through the body, the texture of objects against skin, or the subtle play of weight and balance during movement all offer pathways back to immediate experience. These sensory connections ground abstract thoughts in concrete reality.

Nature demonstrates present connection effortlessly. Animals and plants exist fully in each moment, responding to immediate circumstances without the burden of projected futures or remembered pasts. Human observers often find their own present awareness awakening in natural settings.

Relationships deepen dramatically when partners practice present connection. Simple activities like sharing a meal become profound experiences when fully attended to. Conversations take on new depth when participants truly listen rather than planning their next response.

Work performance improves with present connection. Tasks completed with full attention show higher quality and fewer errors than those done while multitasking. Creative solutions often emerge when minds fully engage with current challenges rather than rushing toward future goals.

Food tastes different when eaten with present awareness. Flavors and textures reveal subtle qualities usually missed during distracted eating. This enhanced perception often leads to more satisfying meals and better nutritional choices.

Children naturally excel at present connection until cultural conditioning teaches them to prioritize past and future. Observing young people at play provides powerful lessons in immediate engagement with life. Their spontaneous joy demonstrates the rewards of full presence.

Urban environments challenge present connection with constant stimulation and demands for attention. Successfully maintaining presence amid city life requires intentional practice and regular renewal through quiet moments and natural settings.

Movement practices like dance, martial arts, or athletics develop present connection through necessity. These activities demand full attention to immediate experience for successful performance. Regular engagement in such practices strengthens overall capacity for presence.

Digital technology often disrupts present connection by design. Notifications, updates, and endless scrolling create addictive patterns that pull attention from immediate experience. Mindful technology use becomes essential for maintaining presence in the modern world.

Social gatherings reveal the impact of present connection or its absence. Events where participants maintain genuine presence create memorable experiences and strengthen community bonds. Conversely, disconnected gatherings leave people feeling empty despite surface interactions.

Creative work flourishes with present connection. Artists, writers, and musicians report their best work emerging from states of deep presence with their medium. This focused attention allows direct expression of authentic experience.

Professional relationships transform through present connection. Leaders who maintain presence during interactions build stronger trust and understanding with their teams. Colleagues who practice present listening solve problems more effectively.

Physical health improves with regular present connection. The body's natural healing mechanisms function better when supported by conscious attention. Stress-related ailments often decrease as presence increases.

Sleep quality depends significantly on the ability to maintain present connection while preparing for rest. Racing thoughts about past or future disrupt natural sleep patterns. Evening practices of presence often lead to more restful nights.

Learning accelerates when students maintain present connection with study materials. Information absorbed with full attention integrates more effectively than content reviewed while distracted. Educational outcomes improve with practices that support presence.

Emotional regulation becomes easier through present connection. Feelings observed with immediate awareness often move through naturally, while emotions ignored or suppressed tend to persist and intensify. Present connection provides a foundation for emotional intelligence.

Time perception shifts with present connection. Moments lived fully often feel rich and satisfying regardless of duration. This qualitative experience of time contrasts sharply with the rushed emptiness of disconnected activities.

Decision-making improves through present connection. Choices made with full awareness of current circumstances tend to align better with authentic values than reactions based on past patterns or future fears.

The practice of present connection requires patience and persistence. Like any skill, it develops through regular exercise and gentle correction when attention wanders. The benefits accumulate gradually but profoundly affect all aspects of life.

Success in maintaining present connection comes not from forcing constant awareness but from cultivating the ability to return to presence when distracted. This flexible resilience allows for natural fluctuations while steadily strengthening overall capacity for presence.

Cultivating Authentic Resonance

Authentic resonance emerges when inner truth aligns perfectly with outer expression, creating a harmonic state that others can instantly recognize and trust. Like a well-tuned instrument, people operating from authentic resonance naturally draw others into their frequency of genuine connection.

Sarah discovered this phenomenon during a pivotal presentation to her company's board. After years of carefully scripted performances, she decided to speak from her heart about the project's challenges and her genuine vision for its future. The response was immediate and powerful – board members leaned forward, engaged deeply, and ultimately approved her ambitious proposals.

Research in human behavior demonstrates that people can unconsciously detect authenticity in others within milliseconds of interaction. This instant recognition stems from subtle cues in voice modulation, body language, and emotional congruence that signal genuine expression.

Professional success increasingly depends on authentic resonance. Markets saturated with polished messaging respond powerfully to genuine voices that cut through artificial perfection. Leaders who cultivate authentic resonance build stronger teams and inspire lasting loyalty.

Relationships thrive on authentic resonance. When partners express themselves genuinely, trust develops naturally and communication flows effortlessly. Conflicts resolve more easily when both parties engage from a place of authentic truth rather than defensive posturing.

Creative expression gains depth through authentic resonance. Artists who connect deeply with their genuine experience produce work that touches audiences more profoundly than technically perfect but emotionally distant pieces. This truth applies across all creative fields.

Personal growth accelerates when aligned with authentic resonance. Goals pursued from genuine motivation manifest more easily than those adopted from external pressures. The energy previously spent maintaining facades becomes available for real development.

Cultural influences often challenge authentic resonance by imposing standardized expectations. Breaking free from these constraints requires courage and commitment to personal truth. The reward comes in the form of deeper connections and more meaningful contributions.

Body awareness plays a crucial role in developing authentic resonance. Physical sensations provide honest feedback about alignment with truth. Learning to trust these bodily signals helps maintain authenticity in challenging situations.

Professional environments transform when authentic resonance becomes valued. Teams working from genuine connection accomplish more with less strain. Innovation flows naturally when people feel safe expressing their true insights and concerns.

Educational settings benefit from authentic resonance between teachers and students. Learning deepens when instructors share genuine enthusiasm for their subjects and students feel safe expressing real questions and doubts.

Social media presents unique challenges to authentic resonance. The pressure to create perfect online personas often leads to disconnection from genuine expression. Finding balance requires conscious choice about digital presentation.

Nature connection supports authentic resonance development. Time spent in natural settings helps reset internal authenticity meters often distorted by social conditioning. Regular nature exposure maintains clearer access to genuine expression.

Financial decisions improve with authentic resonance. When choices align with true values rather than external pressures, resources flow more effectively toward meaningful goals. This alignment reduces financial stress and increases satisfaction.

Sleep quality reflects levels of authentic resonance. People living in alignment with their truth generally sleep better than those maintaining inauthentic personas. Dreams often provide guidance toward greater authenticity.

Movement practices reveal authentic resonance through physical expression. Dance, sports, and martial arts allow direct experience of genuine self-expression through body language. These activities develop stronger connection to authentic movement patterns.

Emotional intelligence grows through authentic resonance. Understanding and expressing genuine feelings becomes easier when practicing authentic connection. This emotional clarity supports better relationships and decision-making.

Time management shifts with authentic resonance. Activities aligned with genuine values feel energizing rather than depleting. This natural energy flow creates sustainable productivity without burnout.

Public speaking transforms through authentic resonance. Audiences respond more positively to genuine expression than perfect delivery. Speakers operating from authentic connection create more impactful presentations.

Writing gains power through authentic resonance. Words flowing from genuine experience touch readers more deeply than carefully constructed but artificial prose. This truth applies to all forms of written communication.

Leadership effectiveness multiplies with authentic resonance. Teams naturally align with leaders who demonstrate genuine commitment to shared goals. Trust builds automatically when authority flows from authentic connection.

Conflict resolution improves through authentic resonance. Genuine expression creates space for real understanding between opposing viewpoints. Solutions emerge more easily when all parties engage authentically.

Success in cultivating authentic resonance requires regular practice and self-reflection. Like any valuable skill, it develops through consistent attention and honest self-assessment. The benefits extend far beyond personal development to enhance all areas of life.

The journey toward authentic resonance continues throughout life, offering deeper levels of genuine expression and connection. Each step toward greater authenticity creates ripples of positive influence in all relationships and endeavors.

Breaking Through Defense Mechanisms

Defense mechanisms emerge as protective shields in early life, yet often persist long after their usefulness expires. Like old fortress walls that once protected ancient cities but now restrict growth, these psychological barriers require careful dismantling to allow for personal expansion.

David's story illustrates this common challenge. As a successful executive, he maintained rigid control over his emotions, a pattern developed during a turbulent childhood. While this defense served him well in youth, it now prevented meaningful connections with his family and team members. His journey to break through these barriers began when his daughter asked why he never smiled.

Research in psychology reveals that defense mechanisms operate automatically, often below conscious awareness. These patterns, formed during periods of vulnerability, become deeply ingrained in neural pathways and require conscious effort to reshape.

Physical manifestations of defenses appear in posture, breathing patterns, and muscular tension. The body holds these protective patterns, creating a somatic armor that reflects psychological barriers. Recognition of these physical signs offers a practical starting point for transformation.

Relationships frequently trigger defensive responses, as intimate connections pose perceived threats to established protection systems. Partners often mirror each other's defenses, creating complex dynamics that require mutual awareness and patience to unravel.

Professional settings reveal defense mechanisms through recurring patterns in workplace interactions. Common expressions include perfectionism, procrastination, or excessive self-reliance. Recognizing these patterns allows for more effective leadership and collaboration.

Childhood experiences shape the formation of defense mechanisms. Early interactions with caregivers create templates for protection that influence adult behavior. Understanding these origins helps reduce self-judgment while working through defensive patterns.

Creative expression provides a safe avenue for exploring and transforming defenses. Art, music, and movement can bypass intellectual resistance, allowing gentle contact with protected aspects of self. These approaches often succeed where direct confrontation fails.

Social support plays a crucial role in defense mechanism transformation. Trusted friends and mentors provide secure environments for experimenting with new patterns. Their presence offers safety while exploring vulnerable territory.

Body-based practices help identify and release defensive patterns. Yoga, dance, or martial arts create opportunities to observe protective responses in action. Regular practice develops awareness of both physical and psychological defenses.

Emotional awareness grows as defenses soften. Feelings previously held at bay become accessible, enriching personal experience and deepening relationships. This expanded emotional range supports better decision-making and communication.

Work performance improves when defensive patterns relax. Energy previously spent maintaining protection becomes available for creativity and collaboration. Teams function more effectively as members develop authentic presence.

Nature settings facilitate defense mechanism breakthrough. Natural environments often feel safer than human contexts, allowing defensive patterns to temporarily relax. Regular outdoor experiences support gradual transformation of protective barriers.

Sleep quality reflects the state of psychological defenses. Rigid protection patterns often disrupt natural rest cycles. As defenses soften, sleep typically deepens and becomes more restorative.

Meditation practices reveal defensive patterns through direct observation of mental habits. Regular meditation develops the capacity to recognize and gently release protective responses. This awareness supports lasting transformation.

Communication patterns shift as defenses transform. Authentic expression replaces habitual responses, leading to clearer understanding in all relationships. This improved communication supports both personal and professional growth.

Physical health often improves as psychological defenses release. The body's energy flows more freely when not constrained by protective patterns. This liberation supports natural healing processes and overall wellbeing.

Decision-making becomes clearer without defensive distortion. Choices align more closely with genuine needs and values rather than protective habits. This authenticity leads to more satisfying outcomes in all life areas.

Time perception changes as defenses soften. Present moment experience becomes more accessible without constant protective scanning. This shift allows fuller engagement with current activities and relationships.

Professional guidance through therapy or counseling provides valuable support for defense mechanism transformation. Trained practitioners help identify blind spots and offer tools for working through protective patterns.

Success in breaking through defense mechanisms requires patience and self-compassion. These patterns developed for important reasons and deserve respect even while being transformed. Gentle persistence yields better results than forceful change attempts.

Regular practice in safe settings allows gradual defense mechanism transformation. Small steps in secure environments build confidence for larger changes. This measured approach supports sustainable transformation without overwhelming protective systems.

The journey of breaking through defense mechanisms continues throughout life, offering new levels of freedom and connection. Each step toward greater openness creates opportunities for richer experience and deeper relationships.

Understanding defense mechanisms as natural responses rather than personal failures supports healthy transformation. This compassionate perspective allows for gentle yet persistent work toward greater psychological freedom and authentic expression.

Chapter 5: When Minds Align
The Magic of Mutual Understanding

Mutual understanding creates bridges between hearts and minds, transforming ordinary interactions into profound connections. When two people truly grasp each other's perspectives, a special kind of magic unfolds that transcends conventional communication.

Rachel experienced this transformation during a challenging project with her colleague James. Initially, their different working styles created constant friction. One afternoon, instead of defending her approach, Rachel asked James to explain his concerns. As they shared their underlying motivations and fears, the tension dissolved into a powerful collaboration that elevated their entire team's performance.

Research in interpersonal psychology shows that mutual understanding activates neural pathways associated with empathy and trust. When people feel genuinely understood, their stress levels decrease while their capacity for creative problem-solving expands dramatically.

Cultural differences often present opportunities for developing mutual understanding. When approached with curiosity rather than judgment, these variations become doorways to deeper connection. Each successful bridge built across cultural gaps strengthens the capacity for future understanding.

Family dynamics transform through mutual understanding. Long-standing conflicts often resolve naturally when family members take time to truly comprehend each other's experiences. This healing ripples through generations, breaking cycles of misunderstanding.

Professional relationships flourish with mutual understanding. Leaders who invest time in genuinely understanding their team members create environments where innovation and loyalty thrive naturally. This foundation supports sustainable success beyond simple productivity metrics.

Children demonstrate remarkable capacity for mutual understanding when given appropriate support. Their natural curiosity and openness, when properly nurtured, develop into lasting skills for building connections across differences.

Body language plays a crucial role in developing mutual understanding. Non-verbal cues often communicate more accurately than words, revealing underlying emotions and intentions. Attention to these signals deepens the quality of understanding.

Conflict resolution transforms through mutual understanding. When opposing parties focus first on comprehending each other's positions, solutions often emerge naturally. This approach creates lasting resolutions rather than temporary compromises.

Creative collaboration reaches new heights through mutual understanding. Artists, musicians, and other creators find their work elevated when they deeply comprehend their partners' visions. This synergy produces innovations beyond individual capability.

Educational environments thrive on mutual understanding between teachers and students. When educators grasp their students' perspectives and learners comprehend their teachers' intentions, learning accelerates dramatically.

Intimate relationships deepen through conscious development of mutual understanding. Partners who regularly practice seeing through each other's eyes build resilience against common relationship challenges.

Nature offers lessons in mutual understanding through ecosystem relationships. Observing how different species interact and support each other provides insights for human connection. These natural models inspire more harmonious human relationships.

Workplace efficiency improves significantly with mutual understanding. Teams that invest in comprehending each member's strengths and challenges naturally organize more effectively. This understanding reduces friction and accelerates progress.

Social movements gain power through mutual understanding across different groups. When diverse communities take time to truly comprehend each other's experiences, collective action becomes more focused and effective.

Digital communication requires special attention to mutual understanding. Without physical presence, extra effort must be made to ensure messages are properly understood. This challenge presents opportunities for developing new communication skills.

Emotional intelligence grows through practicing mutual understanding. Regular attempts to comprehend others' feelings naturally enhance overall emotional awareness and regulation.

Time invested in developing mutual understanding pays dividends across all life areas. While initial conversations might take longer, the resulting clarity prevents countless future misunderstandings and conflicts.

Leadership effectiveness multiplies through mutual understanding. When leaders truly comprehend their team members' motivations and challenges, they can create environments that naturally support peak performance.

Global challenges require mutual understanding across nations and cultures. Solutions to worldwide problems emerge more readily when different groups truly comprehend each other's perspectives and needs.

Success in developing mutual understanding requires patience and genuine curiosity. Quick judgments and assumptions must be suspended in favor of open-minded exploration of different viewpoints.

The practice of mutual understanding begins with self-awareness. Understanding one's own perspectives and biases creates space for genuinely comprehending others' viewpoints.

Regular reflection supports the development of mutual understanding. Taking time to consider interactions from others' perspectives builds capacity for future understanding.

The journey toward mutual understanding continues throughout life, offering deeper levels of connection with each step forward. Every effort to truly comprehend another's perspective creates ripples of positive change in all relationships.

Deep Listening and Empathic Presence

The art of deep listening transforms ordinary conversations into sacred exchanges, where understanding flows naturally between hearts and minds. Beyond mere hearing, deep listening engages our full presence and opens pathways to genuine human connection.

Maria discovered this truth during a crisis with her teenage son. Instead of responding with typical parental advice, she chose to listen completely, setting aside her own fears and judgments. As she maintained silent, supportive presence, her son gradually revealed layers of struggle she had never suspected. That evening marked a turning point in their relationship, built on the foundation of truly being heard.

Neuroscience research reveals that deep listening activates multiple brain regions associated with empathy and emotional processing. When someone feels truly heard, their nervous system relaxes, allowing authentic expression to emerge naturally.

Physical posture significantly influences listening quality. An open, receptive body position communicates safety to others while enhancing our own capacity to receive information fully. Simple adjustments in how we sit or stand can dramatically improve listening depth.

Workplace dynamics shift remarkably when deep listening becomes standard practice. Teams that cultivate empathic presence naturally develop stronger collaboration and innovative solutions. Conflicts resolve more easily when all parties feel genuinely heard.

Cultural barriers dissolve through deep listening practices. When people feel safe to express their authentic experiences without judgment, bridges form naturally across demographic differences. This connection creates lasting understanding between diverse groups.

Emotional intelligence develops naturally through regular practice of deep listening. As we attune to others' subtle expressions, our own emotional awareness expands. This growing sensitivity enhances all relationships, personal and professional.

Time perception changes during deep listening. Minutes expand to hold meaningful exchanges, while distractions fade naturally into the background. This altered state allows for deeper connection and understanding.

Nature provides perfect conditions for developing listening skills. The subtle sounds of wind, water, and wildlife train our ears for finer perception. Regular practice in natural settings enhances overall listening capacity.

Partnership dynamics transform through consistent deep listening. When couples practice giving each other complete attention, understanding deepens naturally. Long-standing patterns of conflict often resolve without direct intervention.

Children respond powerfully to deep listening. When adults offer full presence without agenda, young people naturally share their inner worlds. This practice builds trust and emotional security that lasts into adulthood.

Professional effectiveness increases dramatically with improved listening skills. Leaders who master empathic presence naturally inspire trust and loyalty. Team members feel valued and contribute more freely when consistently heard.

Body awareness plays a crucial role in deep listening. Attention to our own physical responses helps maintain presence while receiving others' experiences. This somatic awareness prevents unconscious reactions that might interrupt connection.

Creative expression flows more freely in environments of deep listening. Artists, writers, and innovators find their work enhanced when surrounded by empathic presence. This supportive atmosphere nurtures new ideas and approaches.

Educational outcomes improve significantly when teachers practice deep listening. Students engage more fully with material when they feel genuinely heard. Learning becomes a collaborative journey rather than a one-way transmission.

Digital communication presents unique challenges for maintaining listening presence. Extra attention must compensate for missing physical cues. Conscious practice can help bridge this gap in online interactions.

Conflict resolution transforms through application of deep listening skills. When opposing parties feel fully heard, solutions often emerge naturally. This approach creates lasting harmony rather than temporary compromise.

Healthcare delivery improves with implementation of deep listening practices. Patients share more relevant information when they feel truly heard. Practitioners make better diagnoses through enhanced attention to subtle cues.

Social movements gain strength through deep listening within and between communities. When people feel their experiences are truly received, collective action becomes more focused and effective.

Sleep quality often improves as listening skills develop. The ability to quiet mental chatter and truly receive experience transfers naturally to rest periods. This enhancement supports overall well-being and recovery.

Success in developing deep listening requires regular practice and patience. Like any valuable skill, it grows through consistent attention and application. The benefits extend far beyond immediate interactions.

Meditation practices support development of listening capacity. Regular stillness training enhances ability to maintain presence with others. This foundation supports deeper connections in all relationships.

The journey toward mastery of deep listening continues throughout life, offering new levels of connection and understanding. Each interaction provides opportunity for practice and growth in this essential human skill.

Regular reflection on listening experiences accelerates development. Taking time to consider both successful and challenging exchanges builds capacity for future interactions. This conscious approach supports steady improvement in listening ability.

Building Emotional Bridges

Emotional bridges connect hearts across the chasms of difference, creating pathways for genuine human connection. Like physical bridges that span rivers and valleys, these invisible structures require careful engineering, regular maintenance, and courage to cross.

Sarah discovered this truth while working to rebuild her relationship with her estranged sister. Years of misunderstandings had created a seemingly impassable gulf between them. Beginning with small gestures - a birthday card, a brief text message - she gradually constructed a new connection. Each small step strengthened their bridge until they could finally meet in the middle, their relationship transformed through patient effort.

Psychological research demonstrates that emotional connections form through consistent, small actions rather than grand gestures. These daily choices - a kind word, an attentive glance, a moment of patience - create the foundation for lasting bonds.

Professional relationships flourish when emotional bridges extend beyond formal roles. Leaders who invest in understanding their team members' emotional landscapes create environments where innovation and loyalty naturally thrive. These connections support both individual growth and organizational success.

Cultural differences often present opportunities for emotional bridge-building. When approached with curiosity and respect, these variations become stepping stones rather than barriers. Each successful cross-cultural connection strengthens our capacity for future bridges.

Family dynamics transform through conscious emotional bridge-building. Old wounds begin healing when family members extend understanding across generational gaps. These renewed connections often heal patterns of disconnection that have persisted for generations.

Physical proximity sometimes masks emotional distance. Couples living under the same roof might need to build new bridges of understanding. This process requires courage to acknowledge gaps and patience to construct new connections.

Children naturally excel at emotional bridge-building when given appropriate support. Their innate openness, when nurtured, develops into lasting skills for creating connections across differences. These early experiences shape lifetime patterns of relationship.

Body language plays a crucial role in emotional bridge construction. Non-verbal signals often communicate more effectively than words, creating initial spans across interpersonal gaps. Attention to these subtle cues supports stronger connections.

Workplace harmony depends on well-maintained emotional bridges between team members. When colleagues invest in understanding each other's perspectives, collaboration flows naturally. These professional connections often extend beyond work boundaries.

Creative partnerships thrive on strong emotional bridges. Artists, musicians, and other creators find their work elevated when they build deep understanding with collaborators. These connections spark innovations beyond individual capability.

Nature offers lessons in emotional bridge-building through ecosystem relationships. Observing how different species interact provides insights for human connection. These natural models inspire more harmonious relationship patterns.

Digital communication requires special attention to emotional bridge maintenance. Without physical presence, extra effort must support connection. Creative approaches can help span the digital divide.

Conflict resolution transforms through emotional bridge-building. When opposing parties focus on creating connection before solving problems, solutions emerge naturally. This approach creates lasting harmony rather than temporary peace.

Educational environments thrive on strong emotional bridges between teachers and students. When educators build genuine connections with learners, knowledge transfers more effectively. These relationships often influence lifelong learning patterns.

Time invested in emotional bridge-building pays dividends across all life areas. While initial construction might require significant effort, maintained bridges prevent countless future misunderstandings and conflicts.

Leadership effectiveness multiplies through emotional bridge-building skills. When leaders create genuine connections with team members, organizational culture naturally strengthens. These relationships support sustainable success beyond immediate goals.

Social movements gain power through emotional bridges across different communities. When diverse groups build genuine understanding, collective action becomes more focused and effective. These connections support lasting social change.

Global challenges require emotional bridges across nations and cultures. Solutions to worldwide problems emerge more readily when different groups establish genuine connection. These international bonds support collaborative problem-solving.

Success in emotional bridge-building requires patience and genuine curiosity. Quick judgments and assumptions must yield to careful observation and openness. This approach supports lasting connection rather than superficial agreement.

Regular maintenance ensures emotional bridges remain strong. Like physical structures, these connections require consistent attention and care. Small daily actions support long-term stability.

Trust develops naturally on well-constructed emotional bridges. When people feel safely connected, they share more openly and take appropriate risks. These conditions support both personal and professional growth.

The journey of emotional bridge-building continues throughout life, offering deeper levels of connection with each new span. Every successful bridge creates possibility for future connections, expanding our capacity for relationship.

Self-awareness grounds successful emotional bridge-building. Understanding our own patterns and triggers helps us construct stable connections with others. This foundation supports all relationship efforts.

Shared Consciousness and Collective Experience

Moments of shared consciousness emerge when individuals transcend their separate perspectives to experience a deeper unity. These profound connections shape both personal relationships and larger social movements, creating ripples of transformation that extend far beyond the original participants.

David witnessed this phenomenon during a community music festival when thousands of strangers spontaneously joined voices in an unrehearsed song. The boundary between self and other dissolved as the melody wove through the crowd, creating a temporary but powerful sense of oneness that participants remembered for years afterward.

Research in social psychology reveals that shared experiences activate neural synchronization between participants. When people engage in collective activities, their brain waves often align in patterns that suggest a deeper level of connection than ordinary social interaction.

Traditional cultures have long recognized the power of shared consciousness through ritual and ceremony. These practices create containers for collective experience that strengthen community bonds and support social cohesion. Modern societies often hunger for these deeper connections.

Workplace environments transform when teams access shared consciousness. Projects flow more smoothly, creativity increases, and problems find natural solutions when groups tap into collective wisdom. This phenomenon extends beyond simple cooperation into genuine co-creation.

Family systems heal through moments of shared awareness. When family members experience genuine connection beyond their individual perspectives, old patterns naturally transform. These healing moments often occur during celebrations or times of challenge.

Nature provides powerful settings for collective experience. Groups walking in forests or gathering by oceans often report spontaneous feelings of connection that transcend ordinary awareness. These experiences frequently catalyze environmental awareness and action.

Creative collaborations reach new heights through shared consciousness. Musicians, dancers, and other artists describe moments when individual expression merges into collective creation. These experiences often produce work beyond any single person's capability.

Sports teams demonstrate shared consciousness during peak performance. Players describe knowing teammates' movements without looking, acting as one organism rather than separate individuals. These states often correlate with exceptional achievements.

Educational settings come alive when students and teachers access collective awareness. Learning becomes an organic, shared exploration rather than a transfer of information. These experiences often inspire lifelong curiosity and connection.

Crisis situations sometimes catalyze spontaneous shared consciousness. Communities responding to natural disasters or other challenges often report extraordinary experiences of unity and collective purpose. These moments frequently inspire lasting social change.

Digital technology presents new opportunities for shared experience across physical distance. While different from in-person connection, online communities can generate powerful collective awareness. These virtual spaces require intentional cultivation.

Meditation practices often lead to experiences of shared consciousness. Groups practicing together regularly report sensing a field of awareness that extends beyond individual minds. These experiences frequently inspire deeper spiritual exploration.

Professional conferences transform when participants move beyond networking into genuine collective experience. Ideas flow more freely, connections deepen, and new possibilities emerge through shared awareness. These moments often spark innovation across entire fields.

Children naturally access shared consciousness during play. Their spontaneous capacity for collective imagination offers lessons for adults seeking deeper connection. This natural ability often fades without conscious cultivation.

Scientific research increasingly supports ancient wisdom about collective consciousness. Studies in quantum physics and consciousness research suggest deeper connections between minds than previously recognized by Western science.

Leadership effectiveness multiplies through ability to foster shared awareness. When leaders create conditions for collective experience, organizations naturally align toward common purpose. This alignment supports sustainable success beyond individual effort.

Social movements gain power through shared consciousness. When diverse groups access collective awareness, their actions become more coordinated and effective. These experiences often sustain long-term commitment to change.

Conflict resolution transforms through moments of shared awareness. When opposing parties experience genuine connection, solutions emerge naturally from collective wisdom. These resolutions tend to last longer than negotiated compromises.

Time perception shifts during experiences of shared consciousness. Participants often report a sense of timelessness or altered temporal awareness. These experiences can create lasting bonds between those present.

Body awareness plays a crucial role in accessing collective experience. Physical sensations often provide the first indication of shifting into shared consciousness. Attention to these cues can help cultivate and maintain collective states.

Regular practice develops capacity for shared consciousness. Like any skill, ability to access and maintain collective awareness grows through consistent attention. Communities that prioritize these experiences often demonstrate remarkable resilience.

Success in fostering shared consciousness requires balance between structure and spontaneity. Too much control prevents natural emergence, while too little support may miss opportunities for deeper connection. This balance develops through experience.

The journey into shared consciousness continues throughout life, offering new depths of connection and understanding. Each experience builds capacity for future collective awareness, expanding human potential for genuine unity.

The Power of Emotional Synchronicity

Emotional synchronicity creates invisible threads that weave people together in profound and meaningful ways. Like musicians finding perfect harmony, humans naturally attune to each other's emotional frequencies when given proper conditions and awareness.

Lisa experienced this phenomenon during a grief support group meeting. As participants shared their stories, the room's emotional atmosphere shifted into perfect alignment. Without words, each person felt the others' pain and healing, creating a powerful resonance that transcended individual experiences. This synchronicity provided more healing than years of individual therapy.

Research in interpersonal neurobiology shows that human nervous systems naturally attempt to synchronize when people spend time together. This biological tendency supports emotional bonding and creates foundations for deeper relationships. Studies reveal that mothers and infants automatically match heart rhythms and breathing patterns during nurturing interactions.

Professional teams achieve remarkable results when they develop emotional synchronicity. Beyond mere cooperation, this alignment allows groups to anticipate needs and respond fluidly to challenges. Sports teams call this being "in the zone," while musicians refer to it as "finding the groove."

Cultural ceremonies and rituals historically served to create emotional synchronicity within communities. Traditional dances, songs, and gatherings aligned people's emotional states, building stronger social bonds. Modern societies often lack these crucial synchronizing experiences.

Family dynamics transform when members achieve emotional alignment. Daily routines become smoother, conflicts resolve more easily, and support flows naturally when families develop synchronicity. This harmony often extends to influence future generations.

Nature provides perfect settings for developing emotional synchronicity. Groups walking in forests or gathering by oceans often experience spontaneous emotional alignment. These shared experiences in natural settings create lasting bonds between participants.

Workplace productivity soars when teams maintain emotional synchronicity. Projects flow smoothly, creativity flourishes, and problems find natural solutions when groups achieve this state. Leaders who understand this principle cultivate environments that support emotional alignment.

Creative collaborations reach extraordinary levels through emotional synchronicity. Artists working together often describe moments when individual expressions merge into perfect harmony. These experiences frequently produce breakthrough innovations.

Educational environments thrive on emotional alignment between teachers and students. Learning becomes effortless when educational groups achieve synchronicity. These harmonious states support deeper understanding and retention.

Physical proximity amplifies opportunities for emotional synchronicity. While technology enables connection across distances, in-person interactions provide richer opportunities for emotional alignment. Body language and subtle energetic cues support this process.

Couples who develop strong emotional synchronicity report more satisfying relationships. Their ability to attune to each other's emotional states creates deeper intimacy and understanding. This alignment helps navigate challenges and celebrate joys together.

Children naturally excel at emotional synchronicity when given supportive environments. Their spontaneous capacity for emotional alignment offers lessons for adults seeking deeper connections. This natural ability requires nurturing to maintain into adulthood.

Professional counseling and therapy work through principles of emotional synchronicity. Skilled practitioners align with clients' emotional states to create healing environments. This therapeutic alignment supports transformation and growth.

Social movements gain momentum through emotional synchronicity among participants. When groups achieve emotional alignment around shared purposes, their collective actions become more powerful and effective. This harmony sustains long-term commitment to causes.

Time perception shifts during states of emotional synchronicity. Participants often report feeling perfectly present together, neither rushing ahead nor lagging behind. These aligned experiences create memorable moments of connection.

Leadership effectiveness depends heavily on ability to create emotional synchronicity within groups. When leaders successfully align team emotions, coordination happens naturally. This alignment supports sustainable organizational success.

Conflict resolution transforms through emotional synchronicity. When opposing parties achieve emotional alignment, solutions emerge organically. This harmony creates lasting resolutions rather than temporary compromises.

Digital communication requires extra attention to maintain emotional synchronicity. While technology can support connection, users must consciously work to create emotional alignment across digital platforms. New tools and practices continue evolving to support this need.

Success in developing emotional synchronicity requires patience and practice. Like learning to dance or play music together, groups must invest time in developing this capability. Regular practice strengthens capacity for emotional alignment.

Physical exercise and movement support development of emotional synchronicity. Group activities like dance, sports, or martial arts create opportunities for practicing emotional alignment. These embodied experiences build lasting capacity for synchronicity.

The journey toward emotional synchronicity continues throughout life, offering new depths of connection and understanding. Each experience of alignment builds capacity for future synchronicity, expanding human potential for harmony.

Regular reflection enhances development of emotional synchronicity. Taking time to consider both successful and challenging experiences helps refine ability to create alignment. This conscious approach supports steady improvement in emotional attunement.

Chapter 6: Healing Through Resonance

Therapeutic Applications of Limbic Bonding

Limbic bonding represents one of the most powerful healing mechanisms available in therapeutic settings. This deep neurological connection between humans can transform trauma, heal attachment wounds, and create lasting positive change in ways that conventional therapeutic approaches alone cannot achieve.

Maria, a skilled therapist, witnessed this transformation while working with a traumatized teenager. Through careful attunement and presence, she established a limbic connection that allowed the young client to feel truly safe for the first time since childhood. This neurological bridge became the foundation for profound healing that talk therapy alone had not accomplished.

Research in interpersonal neurobiology reveals that limbic bonding activates specific neural pathways associated with healing and growth. When two people achieve this deep connection, their nervous systems begin to regulate each other, creating opportunities for repair of early developmental wounds.

Professional therapeutic relationships transform through intentional cultivation of limbic bonds. Rather than maintaining rigid boundaries, skilled practitioners learn to create safe connection while maintaining appropriate professional ethics. This balance supports deeper healing while protecting both client and therapist.

Group therapy settings provide unique opportunities for multiple limbic bonds to form simultaneously. Participants often experience accelerated healing through these interconnected relationships, as each positive connection strengthens the overall therapeutic field.

Family therapy benefits particularly from understanding limbic bonding processes. When family members learn to establish healthy neurological connections, old patterns of dysfunction naturally transform. These new patterns often persist long after therapy ends.

Trauma recovery accelerates when practitioners understand and utilize limbic bonding principles. Rather than focusing solely on narrative or cognitive approaches, therapy incorporating limbic connection addresses deeper neurological patterns of distress.

Children respond remarkably well to therapeutic approaches based on limbic bonding. Their natural capacity for connection, when met with skilled therapeutic presence, creates rapid positive change. These early interventions often prevent later psychological difficulties.

Couples therapy reaches new depths through intentional cultivation of limbic bonds. Partners learn to establish and maintain healthy neurological connection, creating lasting positive change in their relationship patterns. This approach addresses issues at their neurological root.

Educational therapy and specialized learning support benefit from limbic bonding principles. Students with learning differences often show marked improvement when working with practitioners who establish strong neurological connection. This approach supports both academic and emotional growth.

Crisis intervention becomes more effective when practitioners understand limbic bonding. Quick establishment of neurological safety through connection helps stabilize acute situations. These brief but powerful interventions often prevent further trauma.

Addiction recovery programs strengthen through incorporation of limbic bonding principles. When participants experience healthy connection, their need for chemical regulation often decreases. These neurological bonds support long-term sobriety.

Grief counseling transforms through understanding of limbic connection. Rather than rushing to process loss cognitively, skilled practitioners create safe space for neurological co-regulation. This approach supports natural grieving processes.

Professional supervision benefits from limbic bonding awareness. When supervisors establish strong neurological connection with supervisees, learning and growth accelerate. This approach creates more effective therapeutic practitioners.

Physical therapy and bodywork integrate limbic bonding principles for enhanced results. Practitioners who understand neurological connection achieve better outcomes than those focusing solely on physical technique. This holistic approach supports comprehensive healing.

Psychiatric care improves through attention to limbic bonding. While medication plays an important role, establishing healthy neurological connection often reduces necessary dosages. This balanced approach supports optimal treatment outcomes.

Elder care transforms through application of limbic bonding principles. When caregivers establish strong neurological connection, elderly clients show improved physical and emotional outcomes. These relationships support dignity in aging.

Developmental therapy for children with special needs benefits particularly from limbic bonding approaches. When practitioners establish strong neurological connection, development often accelerates across multiple domains. These improvements frequently exceed expected outcomes.

Success in therapeutic limbic bonding requires ongoing professional development. Practitioners must constantly refine their ability to establish and maintain healthy connection while managing their own nervous system states. This balance supports sustainable practice.

Research continues revealing new applications for limbic bonding in therapeutic settings. From traditional psychotherapy to innovative treatment approaches, understanding neurological connection enhances effectiveness across modalities. These discoveries expand therapeutic possibilities.

Time invested in establishing limbic bonds pays significant dividends in therapeutic outcomes. While initial connection may require patience, the resulting neurological safety accelerates overall treatment progress. This investment supports efficient therapy.

Regular supervision and personal therapy help practitioners maintain healthy limbic bonding capacity. Like any therapeutic tool, ability to establish and maintain neurological connection requires ongoing maintenance. This support ensures ethical and effective practice.

The future of therapy increasingly recognizes the central importance of limbic bonding. As research continues confirming its effectiveness, more training programs incorporate these principles. This evolution enhances therapeutic practice across all specialties.

Relationship Repair and Recovery

Healing wounded relationships requires courage, patience, and skilled navigation through complex emotional territories. When trust breaks down or connection frays, specific approaches can help restore and sometimes even strengthen the bonds between people.

Sarah and Michael's marriage teetered on the brink of collapse after Michael's emotional affair with a coworker. Through dedicated work with a relationship counselor, they

learned that repair wasn't just about addressing the affair –
it required rebuilding their fundamental patterns of
connection. Their journey illustrates key principles of
relationship recovery.

Research shows that successful relationship repair follows
predictable patterns. The first crucial step involves creating
safety for both parties to express hurt without fear of
retaliation or dismissal. This foundation of emotional
security allows genuine healing to begin.

Trust rebuilding occurs gradually through consistent, small
actions rather than grand gestures. Each kept promise, each
moment of emotional availability, and each demonstration
of changed behavior adds another brick to the rebuilding
process. Quick fixes rarely create lasting change.

Effective communication during repair requires new skills.
Partners must learn to express needs clearly while
remaining open to hearing difficult truths. The practice of
reflective listening, where each person accurately mirrors
back what they've heard, proves particularly valuable
during this phase.

Forgiveness emerges as a process rather than a single
decision. Those who have been hurt need time to process
their emotions, while those who caused harm must
demonstrate genuine remorse through changed behavior.
Rushing this process often leads to superficial repair that
doesn't last.

Physical proximity plays a crucial role in relationship
recovery. While some separation may be necessary

initially, healing typically requires regular face-to-face interaction. These encounters allow nervous systems to re-regulate and rebuild safety in each other's presence.

Understanding the impact of past trauma helps guide the repair process. Many relationship ruptures trigger old wounds, making current conflicts more intense than the situation warrants. Recognizing these patterns helps partners respond more effectively to each other's needs.

Practical strategies for rebuilding trust include establishing clear agreements, maintaining transparency, and following through on commitments. Each successful interaction builds confidence in the relationship's potential for renewal.

Children affected by relationship rupture need special consideration during the repair process. Their sense of security often depends on adult relationships, making careful attention to their needs crucial for family healing.

Professional support frequently proves invaluable during relationship recovery. Skilled therapists help navigate complex emotions while teaching practical tools for rebuilding connection. This guidance often shortens the repair process significantly.

Timing matters significantly in relationship repair. Attempting deep emotional work before establishing basic safety usually proves counterproductive. Understanding this sequence helps partners pace their healing process appropriately.

Group support can provide valuable perspective during relationship recovery. Whether through formal therapy groups or informal friendships, hearing others' experiences of successful repair offers hope and practical guidance.

Physical touch requires careful consideration during relationship healing. While appropriate touch can help rebuild connection, partners need clear agreements about boundaries and consent. Respecting these boundaries supports the restoration of trust.

Setbacks occur naturally during the repair process. Understanding this prevents discouragement when old patterns temporarily resurface. Each setback provides opportunities for practicing new skills and deepening understanding.

Regular relationship maintenance prevents many problems from escalating to crisis levels. Partners who check in regularly and address small issues promptly often avoid major ruptures entirely.

Cultural factors influence relationship repair strategies. Understanding how different backgrounds affect expectations and communication styles helps partners navigate recovery more effectively.

Work relationships require specific approaches to repair. Professional boundaries and organizational contexts need consideration while rebuilding trust and connection in workplace settings.

Digital communication plays an increasing role in relationship recovery. While face-to-face interaction remains crucial, thoughtful use of technology can support the healing process between meetings.

Self-care becomes essential during relationship repair work. Partners need to maintain their individual well-being while engaging in the challenging work of rebuilding connection.

Success in relationship repair often requires patience with the process. While some improvements may appear quickly, deep healing typically takes consistent effort over time.

Future prevention strategies emerge naturally from successful repair work. Partners who have navigated recovery successfully often develop stronger skills for maintaining healthy connection going forward.

The investment in relationship repair yields benefits beyond the specific relationship being healed. Skills learned during this process typically improve all relationships in each person's life.

Regular reflection helps partners recognize progress that might otherwise go unnoticed. Acknowledging small improvements supports motivation for continuing the healing journey.

Collective Healing in Community

Communities possess remarkable healing potential when members unite with shared purpose and understanding. Throughout history, collective healing has transformed trauma, strengthened social bonds, and rebuilt broken societies.

A small town in Minnesota demonstrated this power after a devastating flood destroyed many homes. Rather than allowing individual families to struggle alone, the community organized shared rebuilding efforts. Through collective action, they not only restored physical structures but also strengthened social connections that sustained them through future challenges.

Research consistently shows that collective healing processes achieve outcomes far beyond what individuals can accomplish alone. When groups work together to address shared wounds, they create resilient support networks that continue providing benefits long after initial healing occurs.

Traditional cultures have long understood the importance of community healing rituals. From grieving ceremonies to celebration gatherings, these practices help process collective emotions and restore group harmony. Modern societies often benefit from adapting these time-tested approaches.

Neighborhood initiatives demonstrate how local communities can facilitate healing. Simple actions like community gardens, shared meals, or regular gatherings create opportunities for connection and mutual support. These ongoing activities build foundations for deeper healing work.

Schools play crucial roles in collective healing processes. When educational communities address shared challenges together, they create safer environments for learning and growth. These efforts often extend positive influences into surrounding neighborhoods.

Religious and spiritual communities traditionally served as centers for collective healing. While specific beliefs vary, the practice of coming together for mutual support and renewal spans cultures and traditions. These gatherings often provide essential emotional safety nets.

Workplace communities benefit significantly from collective healing approaches. Organizations that address shared challenges together develop stronger teams and more resilient cultures. This collaborative healing supports both individual and group success.

Natural disasters often catalyze powerful collective healing responses. Communities that work together through crisis recovery typically emerge stronger than those where individuals cope alone. These experiences create lasting bonds between participants.

Cultural arts provide powerful tools for collective healing. Through music, dance, visual arts, and storytelling, communities process shared experiences and emotions. These creative expressions often reach people who might resist more formal healing approaches.

Youth groups demonstrate particular sensitivity to collective healing processes. When young people work together to address shared challenges, they develop valuable skills while creating positive change. These experiences often shape lifelong approaches to community engagement.

Environmental restoration projects often serve as vehicles for community healing. As groups work together to repair damaged ecosystems, they simultaneously rebuild human connections. This dual healing of land and community creates lasting positive change.

Sports teams and recreational groups provide natural settings for collective healing. Through shared physical activity and common goals, these groups often process deeper emotional experiences. The combination of movement and connection supports effective healing.

Professional associations can facilitate important collective healing work. When industry groups address shared challenges together, they create stronger support networks for all members. These efforts often improve entire professional fields.

Digital communities increasingly contribute to collective healing processes. While online connection cannot fully replace physical presence, virtual groups provide valuable support and resources. These digital networks often complement local healing efforts.

Intergenerational healing requires special attention in community settings. When different age groups work together, they share wisdom and experience that enriches everyone involved. These connections help break cycles of generational trauma.

Leadership development strengthens through collective healing approaches. When communities invest in growing new leaders, they create sustainable foundations for ongoing support and development. This investment ensures continuity of healing resources.

Conflict resolution transforms through community-based approaches. When groups learn to address differences collectively, they develop stronger problem-solving capabilities. These skills continue benefiting communities long after initial conflicts resolve.

Economic challenges often trigger collective healing responses. Communities that address financial hardships together typically develop more resilient local economies. These collaborative solutions create sustainable prosperity.

Health crises demonstrate the essential nature of collective healing. When communities unite to address medical challenges, they achieve better outcomes than isolated efforts. These experiences often lead to improved healthcare systems.

Regular celebration strengthens collective healing processes. Communities that acknowledge progress and honor achievements maintain momentum for positive change. These celebrations help sustain long-term healing efforts.

Documentation of collective healing experiences provides valuable resources for other communities. When groups share their successes and challenges, they help others navigate similar situations. This knowledge sharing accelerates healing across different locations.

Success in collective healing requires ongoing commitment and attention. Communities must regularly renew their dedication to working together for positive change. This consistent effort maintains healing momentum while preventing regression to old patterns.

Chapter 7: The Future of Human Connection

Evolution of Emotional Intelligence

Emotional intelligence emerges through distinct developmental stages, shaped by experiences, relationships, and conscious effort toward growth. Understanding this evolution helps individuals recognize their current capacities while identifying paths for further development.

Consider Maya, a successful executive who struggled with emotional awareness in her early career. Through dedicated practice and mentorship, she transformed her ability to recognize and respond to both her own emotions and those of others. Her journey illustrates key principles in emotional development.

Research reveals that emotional intelligence begins developing in infancy through attunement with caregivers. These early experiences create neural patterns that influence emotional processing throughout life. However, the brain's plasticity allows for continued growth and adaptation well into adulthood.

Childhood experiences significantly shape emotional development. Children who receive consistent emotional validation and guidance typically develop stronger foundations for future growth. Yet even those with challenging early experiences can develop robust emotional intelligence through later intervention and practice.

Adolescence marks a crucial period in emotional development as the brain undergoes significant reorganization. During this time, individuals develop more sophisticated emotional awareness and regulation capabilities. Support during this phase proves particularly valuable for long-term emotional intelligence.

Cultural factors deeply influence emotional intelligence development. Different societies emphasize various aspects of emotional awareness and expression, creating diverse paths for growth. Understanding these cultural influences helps individuals navigate their own developmental journey.

Professional environments present unique opportunities for emotional intelligence growth. Workplace challenges often catalyze development of more sophisticated emotional skills. These experiences contribute significantly to overall emotional maturity.

Relationship experiences powerfully shape emotional intelligence evolution. Each significant connection provides opportunities for developing greater emotional awareness and skill. These interpersonal laboratories offer essential practice grounds for growth.

Stress and challenge, while potentially difficult, often accelerate emotional intelligence development. Individuals who successfully navigate challenging situations typically emerge with enhanced emotional capabilities. These growth opportunities require proper support and resources.

Physical health significantly influences emotional intelligence development. Regular exercise, adequate sleep, and proper nutrition support optimal emotional processing. Understanding these connections helps individuals create conditions for growth.

Meditation and mindfulness practices contribute substantially to emotional intelligence evolution. Regular practitioners often demonstrate enhanced emotional awareness and regulation abilities. These practices provide valuable tools for ongoing development.

Educational experiences shape emotional intelligence in both formal and informal settings. Teachers who model emotional intelligence while providing opportunities for practice support student development. These learning environments create lasting positive impact.

Leadership roles often catalyze rapid emotional intelligence growth. The challenges of guiding others require enhanced emotional awareness and skill. This development typically benefits all aspects of life.

Parenting experiences provide powerful opportunities for emotional intelligence evolution. The daily challenges of raising children often trigger accelerated emotional growth. This development supports both parenting effectiveness and general life success.

Creative expression facilitates emotional intelligence development through various channels. Artists often develop sophisticated emotional awareness through their work. These creative processes offer valuable growth opportunities for everyone.

Technology increasingly influences emotional intelligence evolution. Digital interactions present new challenges and opportunities for emotional skill development. Understanding these influences helps optimize technology use for growth.

Social movements often trigger collective emotional intelligence development. When groups work together for change, they typically develop enhanced emotional capabilities. These experiences create lasting positive impact.

Crisis situations, while challenging, often accelerate emotional intelligence growth. Individuals who successfully navigate difficulties usually emerge with stronger emotional skills. Proper support during these times proves crucial for positive development.

Regular reflection practices support ongoing emotional intelligence evolution. Individuals who consistently examine their emotional experiences typically develop greater awareness and skill. These habits create foundations for continued growth.

Professional development programs increasingly recognize the importance of emotional intelligence training. Organizations that invest in these areas typically see improved performance and satisfaction. These initiatives support both individual and collective growth.

Mentorship relationships provide valuable support for emotional intelligence development. Experienced guides help navigate challenges while modeling advanced emotional skills. These connections often catalyze significant growth.

Research continues revealing new aspects of emotional intelligence development. Scientific understanding helps create more effective growth strategies. This knowledge supports both individual and professional development programs.

Success in emotional intelligence evolution requires sustained commitment. Regular practice and reflection support ongoing growth. This dedication typically yields significant life benefits.

The future of emotional intelligence development increasingly recognizes its crucial role in human success. As understanding grows, new approaches emerge to support this essential aspect of human development. These advances benefit individuals and societies alike.

Age brings unique opportunities for emotional intelligence growth. Mature individuals often develop more nuanced emotional understanding through life experience. This development continues throughout the lifespan when properly supported.

Technology and Emotional Bandwidth

Digital connections increasingly interweave with our emotional experiences, creating new challenges and opportunities for maintaining authentic human relationships. The constant flow of information and interaction demands careful attention to preserve our emotional bandwidth while leveraging technology's benefits.

Lisa, a remote team leader, discovered this balance through trial and error. Initially overwhelmed by constant digital communications, she developed strategies to protect her emotional energy while maintaining strong virtual connections with her team. Her experience highlights crucial aspects of managing technology's impact on our emotional capacity.

Research indicates that human brains process digital interactions differently from face-to-face encounters. While technology enables unprecedented connectivity, it can drain emotional resources more quickly than traditional interactions. Understanding these differences helps create sustainable digital habits.

Social media platforms present particular challenges for emotional bandwidth management. The constant exposure to others' curated lives and opinions can overwhelm natural emotional processing capabilities. Strategic approach to these platforms proves essential for maintaining psychological well-being.

Video conferencing brings unique demands on emotional energy. While enabling valuable connection, these interactions require more intense focus and emotional labor than in-person meetings. Recognizing these costs helps structure virtual interactions more effectively.

Message notifications create ongoing interruptions that fragment emotional attention. Each alert triggers a small emotional response, potentially depleting overall capacity throughout the day. Managing these interruptions becomes crucial for preserving emotional resources.

Digital boundaries require conscious cultivation in our connected world. Setting clear limits on technology use helps protect emotional bandwidth for essential relationships and activities. These boundaries often need regular adjustment as circumstances change.

Sleep quality suffers significantly from unmanaged technology use. Evening screen time can disrupt natural sleep patterns, reducing emotional resilience the following day. Creating technology-free periods before bedtime supports emotional well-being.

Work-life balance faces new challenges in our digital age. When work communications can reach us anywhere, protecting personal time requires deliberate effort. Clear agreements about availability help preserve emotional energy for both professional and personal life.

Physical movement often decreases with increased technology use. Regular exercise proves essential for maintaining emotional capacity, requiring conscious effort in our digital world. Integrating movement throughout the day supports sustainable emotional bandwidth.

Relationship dynamics transform through digital mediation. While technology enables frequent contact, maintaining deep emotional connections requires intentional effort. Understanding these dynamics helps create meaningful digital interactions.

Children's emotional development faces unique challenges in our connected world. Young people need guidance in managing technology while developing essential emotional skills. Parents must model healthy digital habits while supporting organic emotional growth.

Creative expression often suffers from constant digital engagement. Making space for offline creativity helps maintain emotional freshness and resilience. These breaks from technology support overall emotional well-being.

Professional collaboration requires new approaches in digital environments. Teams must learn to build trust and maintain emotional connection through virtual channels. Effective strategies combine technology use with attention to human needs.

Cultural differences influence technology's impact on emotional bandwidth. Various societies approach digital interaction differently, affecting emotional demands and expectations. Understanding these variations helps navigate global connections.

Digital detox periods provide essential recovery for emotional resources. Regular breaks from technology allow natural emotional rhythms to reset. These interruptions often enhance overall productivity and well-being.

Mindfulness practices help maintain emotional awareness amid digital distractions. Simple techniques for staying present support better technology management. Regular practice builds capacity for maintaining balance.

Information overload directly impacts emotional bandwidth. Carefully curating digital inputs helps preserve emotional energy for important matters. Strategic consumption supports sustainable emotional capacity.

Virtual communities can either drain or support emotional resources. Choosing engaging digital connections while limiting draining ones helps maintain emotional health. These choices require regular reassessment as needs change.

Physical space design influences technology's emotional impact. Creating designated areas for focused work and digital-free relaxation supports better balance. These environmental choices affect daily emotional capacity.

Time management transforms when considering emotional bandwidth. Traditional productivity approaches often fail to account for technology's emotional costs. New strategies must incorporate these hidden demands.

Future planning must consider technology's role in emotional well-being. As digital integration increases, maintaining human connection becomes more crucial. Proactive approaches help preserve essential emotional capabilities.

Success in managing technology requires ongoing attention and adjustment. Regular assessment of digital habits helps maintain healthy emotional bandwidth. This maintenance supports both personal and professional effectiveness.

Relationship quality often improves with thoughtful technology management. When digital tools serve human connection rather than replace it, emotional bonds strengthen. This balance creates sustainable patterns for modern life.

The future of emotional well-being increasingly depends on wise technology use. As digital integration continues, protecting and nurturing human emotional capacity becomes essential. Understanding and applying these principles supports thriving in our connected world.

Creating Resonant Spaces

Physical environments profoundly influence our emotional and psychological well-being, shaping how we think, feel, and interact with others. The art of creating resonant spaces combines elements of design, psychology, and human connection to foster environments that nurture both individual growth and collective harmony.

Sarah, an educational consultant, transformed a struggling inner-city classroom by redesigning its physical layout and introducing natural elements. The changes dramatically improved student engagement and emotional regulation, demonstrating the powerful impact of thoughtful space design.

Natural light plays a crucial role in creating resonant environments. Research shows that exposure to daylight regulates mood, enhances cognitive function, and promotes overall well-being. Strategic window placement and light management help optimize these benefits throughout the day.

Color psychology influences emotional responses within spaces. Carefully chosen palettes can promote calm, stimulate creativity, or enhance focus depending on the environment's purpose. Understanding these effects helps create spaces that support intended activities and emotional states.

Acoustic design significantly affects how people experience spaces. Managing sound through materials, layout, and architectural elements helps create environments that facilitate both concentration and connection. These considerations become particularly important in shared spaces.

Plant life introduces vital energy into indoor environments. Beyond improving air quality, natural elements reduce stress and enhance cognitive performance. Even small touches of nature can significantly impact space resonance.

Furniture arrangement shapes social interaction patterns. Thoughtful placement can either encourage collaboration or support individual focus. Flexible configurations allow spaces to adapt to changing needs throughout the day.

Material choices influence both physical comfort and psychological well-being. Natural materials often create more welcoming environments than synthetic ones. Texture variety adds sensory richness that enhances space experience.

Traffic flow patterns affect how people move through and use spaces. Well-designed circulation supports natural interaction while preventing congestion. These considerations help spaces function smoothly during peak usage.

Personal space needs vary across cultures and individuals. Creating environments that respect these differences while promoting connection requires careful balance. Flexible boundaries allow users to adjust comfort levels as needed.

Storage solutions significantly impact space functionality. Clean, organized environments reduce cognitive load and promote calm. Thoughtful storage design helps maintain order without sacrificing accessibility.

Temperature regulation affects both physical comfort and cognitive function. Creating consistent thermal environments supports sustained attention and productivity. Individual control options help accommodate varying preferences.

Art integration enhances space resonance through visual interest and emotional engagement. Carefully chosen pieces can inspire, calm, or energize depending on placement and style. Regular rotation keeps environments fresh and engaging.

Technology integration requires careful consideration in resonant spaces. While supporting modern needs, technology should enhance rather than dominate environments. Thoughtful placement helps maintain human-centered spaces.

Transition areas help people shift between different activities and energy levels. Well-designed transitions support psychological preparation for changing tasks or interactions. These spaces prove particularly valuable in busy environments.

Cultural elements contribute to space identity and belonging. Incorporating relevant cultural references helps create inclusive environments. These touches support diverse community engagement.

Maintenance considerations affect long-term space success. Designing for easy upkeep helps preserve environmental quality over time. Regular care routines support sustained space resonance.

Lighting layers create atmospheric flexibility throughout the day. Combining natural and artificial light sources allows spaces to adapt to different needs and times. These variations support natural biological rhythms.

Air quality significantly influences space experience. Proper ventilation and filtration support cognitive function and physical health. Regular monitoring helps maintain optimal conditions.

Scale relationships affect psychological comfort within spaces. Proportional harmony between elements creates subliminal ease. These considerations influence both furniture selection and room layout.

Color temperature changes throughout the day support natural rhythms. Adjustable lighting helps spaces remain appropriate for different activities and times. These variations enhance space functionality.

Views and vistas contribute to psychological well-being. Creating intentional sight lines helps spaces feel more expansive and connected. These elements reduce feelings of confinement.

Biophilic design principles enhance connection with natural patterns. Incorporating organic forms and materials creates inherently welcoming spaces. These approaches support fundamental human needs.

Success in creating resonant spaces requires ongoing attention and adjustment. Regular assessment helps spaces evolve with changing needs. This maintenance ensures sustained environmental effectiveness.

The future of space design increasingly recognizes psychological impact alongside physical function. As understanding grows, new approaches emerge to support human thriving. These developments enhance our ability to create truly resonant environments.

The Global Web of Connection

Interconnectedness shapes our world in increasingly profound ways, weaving together cultures, economies, and human experiences across traditional boundaries. This global web transforms how we understand ourselves and our relationships with others, creating both opportunities and challenges for meaningful connection.

Marcus, a small business owner in rural Kenya, exemplifies this transformation. Through digital platforms, he connected his local artisan cooperative with customers worldwide, not only improving his community's economic prospects but also fostering cultural exchange and understanding. His story demonstrates how global connections can enrich lives while preserving local identity.

Modern transportation networks enable unprecedented physical mobility, allowing people to maintain relationships across vast distances. These connections create complex tapestries of cultural exchange, challenging traditional notions of community while fostering new forms of belonging.

Environmental awareness increasingly shapes our understanding of global interconnection. Actions in one region ripple through ecosystems worldwide, highlighting our shared responsibility for planetary well-being. This recognition drives collaborative efforts for sustainable practices.

Language evolution reflects our interconnected reality. New expressions emerge from cultural mixing, while translation technologies break down communication barriers. These linguistic developments facilitate deeper cross-cultural understanding.

Economic interdependence binds communities worldwide through complex supply chains and financial systems.

Local decisions increasingly consider global implications, requiring broader perspective in daily choices. This awareness transforms business practices and consumer behavior.

Social movements spread rapidly through global networks, inspiring change across borders. Ideas and activism flow between communities, creating powerful waves of collective action. These movements demonstrate humanity's capacity for unified response to shared challenges.

Educational exchange programs build lasting bridges between cultures. Students who study abroad often become lifelong ambassadors for international understanding. These experiences create enduring networks of global citizens.

Cultural festivals celebrate diversity while highlighting common human experiences. These gatherings provide spaces for sharing traditions and building mutual appreciation. Such events strengthen community bonds across cultural differences.

Digital platforms enable instant connection across time zones, transforming how we maintain relationships. While technology cannot replace physical presence, it helps sustain meaningful connections despite distance. These tools require thoughtful use to support genuine human connection.

Food cultures increasingly reflect global influence while maintaining local character. Fusion cuisines demonstrate how traditions can blend creatively, enriching cultural expression. These culinary exchanges facilitate cross-cultural appreciation.

Sports events unite people across national boundaries, creating shared experiences that transcend language barriers. International competitions foster both healthy competition and global cooperation. These gatherings demonstrate humanity's capacity for peaceful interaction.

Art movements flow freely across borders, inspiring new forms of creative expression. Artists increasingly incorporate diverse cultural influences while maintaining authentic voice. This creative exchange enriches global cultural heritage.

Health challenges remind us of our fundamental interconnection. Disease outbreaks and health innovations affect communities worldwide, requiring coordinated response. These situations demonstrate the importance of global cooperation.

Scientific collaboration accelerates through international partnerships. Researchers share findings and resources across borders, advancing human knowledge collectively. These networks demonstrate the power of unified purpose.

Youth culture increasingly reflects global influences while expressing local identity. Young people navigate multiple cultural contexts, creating new forms of expression. Their experiences shape future patterns of global connection.

Traditional wisdom gains new relevance in our interconnected world. Ancient practices offer guidance for maintaining balance amid rapid change. These teachings help navigate contemporary challenges.

Climate patterns highlight our environmental interdependence. Weather events in one region affect communities worldwide, requiring collective response. This reality drives international cooperation efforts.

Music flows freely across cultural boundaries, creating new forms of expression. Artists blend traditions to create unique sounds that reflect global influence. These musical exchanges facilitate cultural understanding.

Humanitarian efforts demonstrate our capacity for global empathy. Communities worldwide respond to disasters and challenges together, showing humanity's collaborative potential. These actions strengthen international bonds.

Trade relationships create complex webs of mutual dependence. Business practices increasingly consider global impact alongside local benefit. This awareness transforms economic decision-making.

Technology infrastructure connects previously isolated communities. Digital access enables participation in global conversations and opportunities. These connections require thoughtful management to support positive outcomes.

Future generations will inherit an increasingly interconnected world. Preparing them for this reality requires new approaches to education and development. Their success depends on understanding and navigating global connections effectively.

Peace initiatives recognize the importance of fostering understanding across differences. Programs that build cross-cultural relationships help prevent conflict and promote cooperation. These efforts support sustainable global harmony.

Success in our interconnected world requires balancing global engagement with local identity. Communities that maintain this balance thrive while contributing to human progress. This approach supports both individual and collective flourishing.